Laughter
Is the Spice
of Life

Laughter
Is the Spice
of Life

W PUBLISHING GROUP
A Division of Thomas Nelson Publishers
Since 1798

www.wpublishinggroup.com

Published by W Publishing Group, a Division of Thomas Nelson, Inc., P.O. Box 141000, Nashville, Tennessee 37214.

Compiled and edited by Beth Ann Patton

Unless otherwise noted, Scripture quotations are from THE NEW KING JAMES VERSION. Copyright © 1979, 1980, 1982, Thomas Nelson, Inc., Publishers.

Scripture quotations noted NIV are from the HOLY BIBLE: NEW INTERNATIONAL VERSION®. Copyright © 1973, 1978, 1984 by International Bible Society. Used by permission of Zondervan Publishing House. All rights reserved.

Scripture quotations noted KJV are from THE KING JAMES VERSION.

"The Baffling Question" and "To the Poorhouse": From FATHERHOOD by Bill Cosby, copyright © 1986 by William H. Cosby, Jr. Used by permission of Doubleday, a division of Random House, Inc.

Library of Congress Cataloging-in-Publication Data

Laughter is the spice of life / edited by Beth Ann Patton.
   p. cm.
   ISBN 0-8499-4472-4
   1. Laughter—Religious aspects—Christianity. I. Patton, Beth Ann.
BT709.L37 2004
242'.02'07—dc22   2003028217

Printed in the United States of America

05 06 07 08 RRD 11 10 9

Laughter is the sun that drives winter from the human face.

—Victor Hugo

Contents

. . . .

CONTENTS

CONTENTS

CONTENTS

Part V: Till Death (or Insanity) Do Us Part
Laughter Is the Spice of Life in Love

Part VI: When the Going Gets Tough . . . All Is Well
Laughter Is the Spice of Life in Adversity

CONTENTS

Part I

A Laugh Is a Smile
That Bursts

••

Laughter Is the Spice of Life

Wrinkles should merely indicate where smiles have been.

—MARK TWAIN

*You don't stop laughing because you grow old;
you grow old because you stop laughing.*

—MICHAEL PRITCHARD

*Among those whom I like or admire, I can find no common
denominator, but among those whom I love, I can: all of
them make me laugh.*

—W. H. AUDEN

A Bit of Sunshine

JOHN WALLACE CRAWFORD

When a bit of sunshine hits ye,
After passing of a cloud,
When a fit of laughter gits ye,
An' yer spine is feelin' proud,
Don't fergit to up and fling it
At a soul that's feelin' blue,
For the minute that ye sling it,
It's a boomerang to you!

Choosing Happiness

• • • • • • • • ANDY ANDREWS • • • • • • • •

Today I will choose to be happy.

Beginning this very moment, I am a happy person, for I now truly understand the concept of happiness. Few others before me have been able to grasp the truth of the physical law that enables one to live happily every day. I know now that happiness is not an emotional phantom floating in and out of my life. Happiness is a choice. Happiness is the end result of certain thoughts and activities, which actually bring about a chemical reaction in my body. This reaction results in a euphoria that, while elusive to some, is totally under my control.

Today I will choose to be happy. I will greet each day with laughter.

Within moments of awakening, I will laugh for seven seconds. Even after such a small period of time, excitement has begun to flow through my bloodstream. I feel different. I am different! I am enthusiastic about the day. I am alert to its possibilities. I am happy!

Laughter is an outward expression of enthusiasm, and I know that enthusiasm is the fuel that moves the world. I laugh through-out the day. I laugh while I am alone, and I laugh in conversation with others. People are drawn to me because I have laughter in my heart. The world belongs to the enthusiastic, for people will follow them anywhere!

Today I will choose to be happy. I will smile at every person I meet.

My smile has become my calling card. It is, after all, the most potent weapon I possess. My smile has the strength to forge bonds, break ice, and calm storms. I will use my smile constantly. Because of my smile, the people with whom I come in contact on a daily basis will choose to further my causes and follow my leadership. I will always smile first. That particular display of a good attitude will tell others what I expect in return.

My smile is the key to my emotional makeup. A wise man once said, "I do not sing because I am happy; I am happy because I sing!" When I choose to smile, I become the master of my emotions. Discouragement, despair, frustration, and fear will always wither when confronted by my smile. The power of who I am is displayed when I smile.

Today I will choose to be happy. I am the possessor of a grateful spirit.

In the past, I have found discouragement in particular situations until I compared the condition of my life to others less fortunate. Just as a fresh breeze cleans smoke from the air, so a grateful spirit removes the cloud of despair. It is impossible for the seeds of depression to take root in a thankful heart.

My God has bestowed upon me many gifts, and for these I will remember to be grateful. Too many times I have offered up the prayers of a beggar, always asking for more and forgetting to give thanks. I do not wish to be seen as a greedy child, unappreciative and disrespectful. I am grateful for sight and sound and breath. If ever in my life there is a pouring out of blessings beyond that, then I will be grateful for the miracle of abundance.

LAUGHTER IS THE SPICE OF LIFE

I will greet each day with laughter. I will smile at every person I meet. I am the possessor of a grateful spirit.

Today I will choose to be happy.

—from *The Traveler's Gift*

Laugh

• • • • • • • NICOLE JOHNSON • • • • • • • •

L *augh*. Laughter works on the soul like medicine. There are a couple of friends that I love going to lunch with. So much healing comes from laughter. We laugh about men, we laugh about longing for heaven. When we finally get around to looking at a menu, we laugh about our longing to be filled. When the waiter comes to take our order, we can hardly get the words out, as one of us invariably orders, "One of everything, please, with cheese." Our longings, as they are discussed with friends, create a bond that wouldn't come if we simply stayed on the surface. Real laughter and enjoyment come from going deep and then rising to the surface to get air. The laughter is the bubbles on the way up. . . .

Laughing with friends is just like eating cake at a party. You can have a party without cake, but who would want to? Every friend I have in my life knows how to belly laugh, and not take themselves, or me, too seriously. Laughter is like a tall, creamy, four-layered, beautiful cake that leans to one side. A cake that is meant to be cut and shared. Two forks and enjoyment beyond belief. It feels great to lose yourself in laughter. Doubled over, knees pressed together so you don't pee, face red, tears rolling down your cheeks. Trying to regain composure, getting serious, and then losing it all over again. Celebration indeed!

—from *Fresh-Brewed Life*

Spontaneous Laughter

SIR WILLIAM OSLER

There is a form of laughter that springs from the heart, heard every day in the merry voice of childhood, the expression of a laughter-loving spirit that defies analysis by the philosopher, which has nothing rigid or mechanical in it, and totally without social significance. . . . Bubbling spontaneously from the heart of child or man, without egotism and full of feeling, laughter is the music of life.

A Formula for Laughter

• • • • • • MARILYN MEBERG • • • • • • • •

Reality-based, positive thinking is a mental habit well worth establishing as an attitude. It produces victory in our daily living, it provides health for our bodies, and it provides cheer for our souls.

Our ability to think positively instead of negatively is first a choice. Proverbs 23:7 states, "For as he thinks in his heart, so is he." Our minds determine who we are, how we behave, and how we feel.

The exciting news about all this is that thoughts come before feelings and before actions. That means we have a lot of control over what we do once we learn to think in godly and positive ways. If we are miserable and unhappy, lacking cheer and lightheartedness, it is possible to change those feelings with healthier thinking.

A Formula for Laughter

I don't usually respond to formulas for this and that; they feel a bit too tidy. But I have developed one for cheerful thinking I'd like to toss your way for your consideration. To begin with, I love to laugh. I believe a giggle is always loitering about even in the most devastating of circumstances. I make a point of shuffling through the rubble in search of that giggle.

This isn't denial. I need to feel and express my pain. But I also need to find the light side—and there is *always* a light side! I've noticed that when I laugh about some minor part of a problem or controversy or worry, the whole situation suddenly seems much less negative to me. After a good laugh, I can then rethink my circumstances. As a result, that which was threatening may now seem less threatening.

Paradoxically, after I've found the giggle, I am more ready to get serious (it's a more balanced seriousness) and consider the degree and the extent of my negative thinking. I pull those negative thoughts up on the screen of my mind and scroll down through the list, considering each one. (Good grief, I just used a computer image!) The value of this is that it's easier to do battle with what I can see; therefore it helps to "look" at these thoughts to determine how logical they are. . . . I now need to determine how I can change those thoughts to realistic optimism. This is when negative thoughts have to be deleted and replaced with those that are realistically positive.

I am convinced that one of life's most easily accessible sources of cheer is to remember some of the off-the-wall, crazy things that happen to us. . . . Sometimes those memories are bittersweet as we recall an out-of-the-ordinary moment with a loved one who is now gone. But those times nevertheless provide cheer because that was the emotion felt when the experience occurred. That original cheerful feeling will always remain attached to that memory.

—from *I'd Rather Be Laughing*

From the Mouths of Babes

• • • • • • • • ANONYMOUS • • • • • • • •

One evening, a father told his five-year-old daughter that she would be disciplined if she got out of bed one more time. She got out of bed. He promptly spanked her. He then consoled her and explained that he did so because he loved her.

As he held her in his lap and wiped the tears from her cheeks, she looked up at his face with big, wet eyes and asked, "Daddy, Jesus died on the cross to pay for all my sins, right?"

"Yes, honey, that's right."

"Okay, then why do I still have to get spanked?"

Playful Pleasures

• • • • • • • • LUCI SWINDOLL • • • • • • • •

*My chosen ones will long enjoy the
works of their hands. (Isaiah 65:22 NIV)*

Playfulness. I love that quality. Playful people look at life through a kaleidoscope lens, seeing all kinds of ways to find adventure and have fun. They've unlocked the door to the child within, and they're always looking for something with which to play—a sight, a sound, a person, an idea. The interesting thing is that they're from all walks of life—the executive, the waitress, the bus driver, the attorney, the gas station attendant, the doctor, the minister, the hairdresser, the street person, and the guy who lives in that high-rise over there.

The child within each of us is the muse for our creativity, the catalyst for our joy, and the spirit behind our wildest dreams. Our inner child wants to dawdle, putter, explore, enjoy, and make up things. It doesn't matter if they are pretty things or formed correctly. What matters is the pleasure that comes as the result of our creative efforts.

With the onslaught of life's demands and duties, some of us forget to be playful. We keep our inner child hidden, "proper" and in line, and we forget that it is she who can provide the enjoyment we long for in daily life. Pablo Picasso put it wisely:

"Every child is an artist. The problem is how to remain an artist once that child grows up." Ah yes! There's the rub.

My adult person has built a little room in my house where my inner child comes out to play: *The Studio*. It is a forty-two-square-foot dream machine. It's painted yellow and crammed full of books, toys, paints, clay, stickers, stamps, and games. It has a small drafting table with chair, a baby radio, and boxes of treasures. Originally, it was the walk-in clothes closet for my bedroom, but how badly do I need a clothes closet? More important, I need a place to play jacks. And I do!

Last night I went in there and blew bubbles. Somebody gave me a little jar of "Miracle Bubbles" with a plastic wand . . . and I blew bubbles for maybe ten minutes. (A few weeks ago I made a new wand with the shape of a cat on the end. I wanted to see if the bubbles would come out cat-shaped. They don't.) That tiny room where I play and paint and putter brings me tremendous pleasure. I'm even branching out now . . . I've taken over the linen closet and pantry for more fun places for Little Luci to have her say. Soon, I'm going into the yard.

Maybe you'd like to have your inner child come outside and enjoy a bit of adventure, but you don't quite know how to coax her forth. After all, you're grown up, have a respectable job where you wear business clothes every day, have worked hard for your education, and don't want to look like an idiot by acting like a child blowing bubbles. You don't have time to be creative and playful. It takes all the energy you can muster just to get through your busy day at the office. If you let down your decorum, what will people think?

I can tell you what they'll think. They'll be jealous that you've found a way to take the drudge out of the daily grind. They'll want to know why you can't wipe that smile off your face. They'll want what you have. They'll ask where you unearthed the fountain of youth and what you're drinking from it. *Everybody wants to be where the fun is.* I don't know a single person who is having too much fun.

Here are a half dozen tips that may help bring your muse into the sunlight:

- Figure out what the child within you wants to do and do it.
- Listen to that tiny, soft voice inside and believe it.
- Quit conforming to what the world demands and say, "No!" (Kids are good at that.)
- Surround yourself with people who love you and enjoy them.
- Create a life for yourself that's meaningful and live there.
- Keep in mind that imagination is more important than knowledge.

These six things won't get you to heaven or make you debt free or fill in all the gaps in your needy soul, but they will give you a start in gaining victory over some of the enemies with which you wage war all too often—boredom, anxiety, cynicism, stress, and procrastination. These little tips have worked for seven decades, and even now I'm still learning about the little person inside me who wants to come out and play.

More than two thousand years ago, Jesus said to a crowd of people gathered around him, "Unless you change and become like little children, you will never enter the kingdom of heaven" (Matthew 18:3 NIV). The truth of that is something we all need to remember today in our busy, rat-race lives.

Don't be afraid to explore playful pleasures in your life. Let them spill outside the bounds of your leisure and work, your home and office, your school and church. Let them permeate your life. And the next time somebody asks for a volunteer to be a clown at the block party, raise your hand.

—from *The Great Adventure*

Child's Play

· · · · · · · LAURA E. RICHARDS · · · · · · · ·

Once a child was sitting on a great log that lay by the road-side, playing; and another child came along, and stopped to speak to him.

"What are you doing?" asked the second child.

"I am sailing to the Southern Seas," replied the first, "to get a cargo of monkeys, and elephant tusks, and crystal balls as large as oranges. Come up here, and you may sail with me if you like."

So the second child climbed upon the log.

"Look!" said the first child. "See how the foam bubbles up before the ship, and trails and floats away behind! Look! the water is so clear that we can see the fishes swimming about, blue and red and green. There goes a parrotfish; my father told me about them. I should not wonder if we saw a whale in about a minute."

"What are you talking about?" asked the second child, peevishly. "There is no water here, only grass; and anyhow this is nothing but a log. You cannot get to islands in this way."

"But we *have* got to them," cried the first child. "We are at them now. I see the palm trees waving, and the white sand glitter-ing. Look! There are the natives gathering to welcome us on the beach. They have feather cloaks, and necklaces, and anklets of copper as red as gold. Oh! and there is an elephant coming straight toward us."

"I should think you would be ashamed," said the second child. "That is Widow Slocum."

"It's all the same," said the first child.

Presently the second child got down from the log.

"I am going to play stick-knife," he said. "I don't see any sense in this, I think you are pretty dull to play things that aren't really there." And he walked slowly away.

The first child looked after him a moment.

"I think *you* are pretty dull," he said to himself, "to see nothing but what is under your nose."

But he was too well mannered to say this aloud; and having taken in his cargo, he sailed for another port.

—from *The Golden Windows*

Sloppy Agape

• • • • • • • PATSY CLAIRMONT • • • • • •

My friend Janet Grant owns a dog named Murphy. Wait, let me try that again. Murphy, a dog, owns my friend Janet. There, that's more accurate.

Murphy is an Australian shepherd; actually, he's still a pup—a very determined, sanguine puppy. *Zealous* doesn't begin to describe his energy, which makes life adventurous for the Grants.

Janet and her hubby, Loch, were making a day trip to visit new friends and decided, at their friends' invitation, to bring Murphy along. They realized they would need to be vigilant lest their joyful live wire and his playful ways overwhelm the homeowners.

Murphy was on his best behavior, but it's difficult to squelch exuberance for long periods of time, and soon Murphy bounded into the living room to present his owners with a gift. Everyone tried not to overreact when they spotted an antique doll dangling from his toothy grin. Janet and Loch breathed a sigh of relief, as did the homeowners, when they were able to retrieve the treasure intact.

Then Murphy decided to be best friends with the homeowner's black Lab, Jill. Only problem was, Jill's friendship card was full, and she was not interested. Murphy's enthusiasm was not diminished. He would sidle up to Jill, who would growl her strong disapproval. Murphy would lay his paw over hers, which really ticked off Jill.

That's when it happened. Jill wasn't about to put up with this adolescent Casanova, especially on her home turf. She took the stance of a predator—front shoulders dropped, ears down. Then she let rip with her fiercest growl, and to drive home her intention to rearrange Murphy's anatomy, she bared her intimidating teeth.

Janet, Loch, and their friends were shocked at what happened next. Instead of backing away, Murphy bounded up into Jill's face. Oblivious to her disgust, Murphy began to lick her teeth. Yes, *her teeth*. Much to everyone's amazement, instead of ripping off Murphy's nose, Jill eased away, and while still not willing to be buddies, from that point on she tolerated Murphy's bubbly presence.

That story makes me giggle. Can't you just see it? Jill gives her best impression of a livid lunatic and receives in return sloppy *agape*.

I had that happen with my kids when they were young. I'd be in a snappy mood, growling around the house, when someone would push me over the edge and I would have a little snarling fit. More than once after a teeth-baring episode, one of my sons would climb into my lap, kiss me, and nuzzle his little head up under my neck. Aww.

The part about Murphy's behavior I love best is his inextinguishable zeal for life and relationships. He just dived in headfirst.

Even though I'm impressed with the indomitable spirit of some, too much happy can be unnerving. Folks who force happy remind me of times when I've worn shoes a size too small and tried to walk as though they fit perfectly. It's so unnatural. But those whose joy is genuine and running over are compelling, right, Jill? Their gladness is an internal, eternal spring that draws people to its Source.

Mary Graham, president of Women of Faith, is that kind of gal. She's an example of compelling joy. She is wise, playful, generous, and relational. Everyone wants to be Mary's best friend, and, gratefully, the Lord has given her an expansive heart; she warmly embraces many. Mary's unassuming ways, her humorous tilt on life, and her commitment to God's truth are thoroughly enjoyable to behold.

Can you think of someone whose life exudes joy? As you think of him or her, what qualities do you see that you admire? Are those qualities a part of your character? Would you like them to be?

Joy is not a private-stock item reserved for the privileged; in fact, it's more like a community pool. All are invited. Dive in!

> Joy of heaven, to earth come down;
> Fix in us Thy humble dwelling;
> All Thy faithful mercies crown!
> Jesus, Thou art all compassion,
> Pure, unbounded love Thou art;
> Visit us with Thy salvation;
> Enter every trembling heart.
> —CHARLES WESLEY
>
> —from *The Great Adventure*

The Best Medicine

• • • • • • • • • ANONYMOUS • • • • • • • • • •

One Sunday a young child was acting up during the morning worship hour. The parents did their best to maintain some sense of order in the pew but were losing the battle. Finally, the father picked the little fellow up and walked sternly up the aisle on his way out.

Just before reaching the safety of the foyer, the little one called loudly to the congregation, "Pray for me! Pray for me!"

While attending a marriage seminar on communication, David and his wife listened to the instructor declare, "It is essential that husbands and wives know the things that are important to each other." He addressed the man: "Can you describe your wife's favorite flower?" David leaned over, touched his wife's arm gently and whispered, "Pillsbury All-Purpose, isn't it?"

Little Johnny asked his grandma how old she was. Grandma answered, "Thirty-nine and holding." Johnny thought for a moment, and then said, "And how old would you be if you let go?"

It was Palm Sunday and because of a sore throat, five-year-old Johnny stayed home from church with his mother. When the rest of his family returned home, they were carrying several palm branches. The boy asked what they were for. "People held them over Jesus' head as He walked by."

"Wouldn't you know it," the boy fumed, "The one Sunday I don't go, He shows up!"

The prospective father-in-law asked, "Young man, can you support a family?" The surprised groom-to-be replied, "Well, no. I was just planning to support your daughter. The rest of you will have to fend for yourselves."

One Sunday morning a minister got up and announced to his congregation: "I have good news and bad news. The good news is, we have enough money to pay for our new building program. The bad news is, it's still out there in your pockets."

A little boy was overheard praying: "Lord, if you can't make me a better boy, don't worry about it. I'm having a real good time like I am."

"The Dog Won't Fly!"

SHEILA WALSH

I t was a new experience for me. I had no idea I would be able to do it. I volunteered out of ignorance, and when the day arrived I was stunned by my naïveté.

"What was I thinking?" I said out loud in the cab as I traveled to the church.

"Can I help you, ma'am?" the driver asked.

"Can you dance?" I replied.

"Not much," he said.

"Well, me neither . . . so now what?"

He returned to concentrating on driving, glad to be about to unload the nut case in the backseat.

It started so innocently. I wanted to write books for children. I actually started writing for my son, and the vision grew into a series of five books published by Waterbrook Press under the banner "Children of Faith." Integrity Music expressed interest in partnering with us, and soon we had a CD. Tommy Nelson caught the vision and we had an animated movie. I was very excited. There was talk of a Christmas tour.

"This will be fun," I said to Barry. "We can all go. Christian has never toured on a bus before. It'll be great. We'll get a tree and lights for the bus and make it a winter wonderland!"

In no time I was sitting at a table with all interested parties.

"Will you be in the tour?" the prospective tour producer asked.

"Sure, if you want me to be," I said too quickly.

"That would be great," he said. And suddenly it was a done deal.

I didn't think much more about it. I was busy with Women of Faith conferences, and Thanksgiving seemed a long way away. But as it edged closer I got the first in a series of unexpected calls.

"We'll need you in Dallas for a week of dance rehearsals. And one week in Nashville, too," the director said.

"Dance rehearsals? Dance rehearsals? What are you talking about? I can't dance. I was raised a Baptist!" I told him, beads of sweat breaking out on my forehead.

"You have the main part of the show," he informed me politely. "The other characters are in large animal costumes. You are our human."

"I don't want to be human. Can't I be the ostrich or monkey?" I begged.

"No."

The cab pulled up outside Prestonwood Baptist Church. The irony did not go unnoticed. I was introduced to the other actors and dancers, all in their twenties. I watched them warm up and stretch in ways I haven't since I gave birth.

"For your first move, bend down, jump as high as you can, and you will end up on my shoulder," Matt said.

"On your shoulder!" I uttered incredulously. "I'm not a parrot."

At the end of the first day and ten hours of jumping around like a maniac squirrel, I was exhausted.

"We're off to the gym, do you want to come?" Julie asked.

"Gym! I want the emergency room!"

Somehow I survived the first week, and as the second week approached its end, opening night reared its ugly head like a date for a root canal. Everything that could go wrong went wrong. Wrong set pieces were delivered, costumes didn't fit; but it all came to a head on the day after Thanksgiving. Opening night was the following evening, and I was still short two pieces of my costume. Have you ever tried to hurry through a mall on the biggest shopping day of the year looking for a purple wig and a feather boa? Suddenly, in the middle of a lynch mob of determined buyers, my cell phone rang.

"The dog won't fly!" the voice cried out.

"What do you mean?" I asked.

"It won't fly. The dog says it's not safe. The dog won't fly!"

I started to laugh. I laughed so hard I had tears running down my face, and I had to hold on to a confused shopper in front of me. She started to laugh; her husband joined in. Soon I was standing in a circle of people who were all laughing and didn't have a clue why.

"Why are we laughing?" the woman asked.

"The . . . the . . . the dog won't fly," I spat out like a sparkler on the Fourth of July. It made no sense to them, but it did wonders for me.

I returned to the set with the wig and boa. We made sure that the dog had enough dance rehearsal time to be comfortable flying. I adjusted the dancing and jumps to fit my forty-five-year-old body, and we had a wonderful time. It was outside my comfort zone. Way outside. But I survived and had so much fun.

How long has it been since you've done something that stretches you? You don't have to be great at it; it's just fun to participate vigorously in life. The dancers in my show got many laughs watching me attempt to land on Matt's shoulder. I never did make it, but I had fun trying.

It's easy to lose joy in life. We get to the stage where we take ourselves too seriously or are afraid to make mistakes. But when we know that we are loved by God, loved beyond measure, we can dive in and take a chance. Success or failure doesn't matter. We showed up, and that's all it takes.

—from *The Great Adventure*

The Prince's Happy Heart

Once upon a time there was a little Prince in a country far away from here. He was one of the happiest little Princes who ever lived. All day long he laughed and sang and played. His voice was as sweet as music. His footsteps brought joy wherever he went. Everyone thought that this was due to magic. Hung about the Prince's neck on a gold chain was a wonderful heart. It was made of gold and set with precious stones.

The godmother of the little Prince had given the heart to him when he was very small. She had said as she slipped it over his curly head: "To wear this happy heart will keep the Prince happy always. Be careful that he does not lose it."

All the people who took care of the little Prince were very careful to see that the chain of the happy heart was clasped. But one day they found the little Prince in his garden, very sad and sorrowful. His face was wrinkled into an ugly frown.

"Look!" he said, and he pointed to his neck. Then they saw what had happened.

The happy heart was gone. No one could find it, and each day the little Prince grew more sorrowful. Then one day he was gone. He had set off on his own to look for the lost happy heart that he needed so much.

The little Prince searched all day. He looked in the city streets and along the country roads. He looked in the shops and in the doors of the houses where rich people lived. Nowhere could he find the heart that he had lost. At last it was almost night. He was very tired and hungry. He had never before walked so far, or felt so unhappy.

Just as the sun was setting the little Prince came to a tiny house. It was very poor and weather-stained. It stood on the edge of the forest. But a bright light streamed from the window. So he lifted the latch, as a Prince may, and went inside.

There was a mother rocking a baby to sleep. The father was reading a story out loud. The little daughter was setting the table for supper. A boy of the Prince's own age was tending the fire. The mother's dress was old. There were to be only porridge and potatoes for supper. The fire was very small. But all the family were as happy as the little Prince wanted to be. Such smiling faces and light feet the children had. How sweet the mother's voice was!

"Won't you have supper with us?" they begged. They did not seem to notice the Prince's ugly frown.

"Where are your happy hearts?" he asked them.

"We don't know what you mean," the boy and the girl said.

"Why," the Prince said, "to laugh and be as happy as you are, one has to wear a gold chain about one's neck. Where are yours?"

Oh, how the children laughed! "We don't need to wear gold hearts," they said. "We all love each other so much, and we play that this house is a castle and that we have turkey and ice cream for supper. After supper mother will tell us stories. That is all we need to make us happy."

"I will stay with you for supper," said the little Prince.

So he had supper in the tiny house that was a castle. And he played that the porridge and potato were turkey and ice cream. He helped to wash the dishes, and then they all sat about the fire. They played that the small fire was a great one, and listened to fairy stories that the mother told. All at once the little Prince began to smile. His laugh was just as merry as it used to be. His voice was again as sweet as music.

He had a very pleasant time, and then the boy walked part of the way home with him. When they were almost to the palace gates, the Prince said, "It's very strange, but I feel just exactly as if I had found my happy heart."

The boy laughed. "Why, you have," he said. "Only now you are wearing it inside."

Laughter Is a Leap

• • • • • • • • G. K. CHESTERTON • • • • • • • •

It is unpardonable conceit not to laugh at your own jokes. Joking is undignified; that is why it is so good for one's soul. Do not fancy you can be a detached wit and avoid being a buffoon; you cannot. If you are the Court Jester you must be the Court Fool. . . .

The fact is that purification and austerity are even more necessary for the appreciation of life and laughter than for anything else. To let no bird fly past unnoticed, to spell patiently the stones and weeds, to have the mind a storehouse of sunsets, requires a discipline in pleasure and an education in gratitude. . . .

For solemnity flows out of us naturally, but laughter is a leap.

For Laughs . . .

The following are headlines collected from local, national, and international newspapers. In each case there is an alternate, more humorous interpretation of the headline.

❀ "Eye Drops Off Shelf"

❀ "Prostitutes Appeal to Pope"

❀ "Kids Make Nutritious Snacks"

❀ "Queen Mary Having Bottom Scraped"

❀ "Dealers Will Hear Car Talk at Noon"

❀ "Milk Drinkers Are Turning to Powder"

❀ "Juvenile Court to Try Shooting Defendant"

❀ "Panda Mating Fails; Veterinarian Takes Over"

❀ "Two Sisters Reunited after Eighteen Years at Checkout Counter"

❀ "Astronaut Takes Blame for Gas in Spacecraft"

❀ "Include Your Children When Baking Cookies"

❀ "Old School Pillars Are Replaced by Alumni"

❀ "Hospitals Are Sued by Seven Foot Doctors"

❀ "Lawmen from Mexico Barbecue Guests"

❀ "Two Soviet Ships Collide, One Dies"

❀ "Red Tape Holds Up New Bridge"

❀ "Iraqi Head Seeks Arms"

❀ "Hershey Bars Protest"

Part II

Mama Knows Best

• •

Laughter Is the Spice of a Mom's Life

*God invented mothers because He couldn't be every-
where at once.*

—JEWISH SAYING

*Somewhere on this globe, every ten seconds, there is a woman
giving birth to a child. She must be found and stopped.*

—SAM LEVENSON

*The best way to keep children home is to make the home
atmosphere pleasant—and let the air out of the tires.*

—DOROTHY PARKER

Laugh Lines

ERMA BOMBECK

My deeds will be measured not by my youthful appearance,
but by the concern lines on my forehead,
the laugh lines around my mouth,
and the chins from seeing what can be done
for those smaller than me or who have fallen.

Job Description

· · · · · · · · · · Anonymous · · · · · · · · · ·

Position: Mother, Mom, Mama, Mommy, Woman!!!

Job Description: Long-term team players needed for challenging permanent work in an often chaotic environment.

- Candidates must possess excellent communication and organizational skills and be willing to work variable hours, which will include evenings and weekends and frequent twenty-four-hour shifts on call.

- Some overnight travel required, including trips to primitive camp sites on rainy weekends and endless sports tournaments in faraway cities. Travel expenses not reimbursed.

- Extensive courier duties also required.

Responsibilities: The rest of your life. Must be willing to be hated, at least temporarily, until someone needs $5. Furthermore:

- Must be willing to bite tongue repeatedly.
- Must possess the physical stamina of a pack mule and be able to go from zero to sixty miles per hour in three seconds flat in case, this time, the screams from the backyard are not someone just crying wolf.

- Must be willing to face stimulating technical challenges, such as small gadget repair, mysteriously sluggish toilets, and stuck zippers.

- Must screen phone calls, maintain calendars, and coordinate production of multiple homework projects.

- Must have ability to plan and organize social gatherings for clients of all ages and mental outlooks.

- Must be willing to be indispensable one minute and an embarrassment the next.

- Must handle assembly and product safety testing of a half million cheap, plastic toys, and battery-operated devices.

- Must always hope for the best, but be prepared for the worst.

- Must assume final, complete accountability for the quality of the end product.

(Responsibilities also include floor maintenance and janitorial work throughout the facility.)

Possibility for Advancement and Promotion: Virtually none. Your job is to remain in the same position for years, without complaining, constantly retraining and updating your skills, so that those in your charge can ultimately surpass you.

Previous Experience: None required unfortunately. On-the-job training offered on a continually exhausting basis.

Wages and Compensation: Get this—you pay them (!), while offering frequent raises and bonuses. A balloon payment is due when they turn eighteen because of the assumption that college will help them become financially independent. When you die, you give them whatever is left.

The oddest thing about this reverse-salary scheme is that you actually enjoy it and wish you could only do more.

Benefits: While no health or dental insurance, no pension, no tuition reimbursement, no paid holidays, and no stock options are offered, this job supplies limitless opportunities for personal growth and free hugs for life *if* you play your cards right.

The Happy Homemaker

• • • • • • • • • ANONYMOUS • • • • • • • • •

An anonymous writer composed a Martha Stewart parody describing the silly extremes people will go to in the name of interior decorating and homemaking. Soon afterward, a fictitious response was added by another mystery writer, making the parody even more hilarious. The fictional correspondence occurs between Martha and humorist Erma Bombeck.

Dear Erma,

This perfectly delightful note is being sent on paper I made myself to tell you what I have been up to. Since it snowed last night, I got up early and made a sled with old barn wood and a glue gun. I handpainted it in gold leaf, got out my loom, and made a blanket in peaches and mauves. Then to make the sled complete, I made a white horse to pull it from DNA that I just had sitting around in my craft room.

By then it was time to start making the placemats and napkins for my twenty breakfast guests. I'm serving the old standard Stewart twelve-course breakfast, but I'll let you in on a little secret: I didn't have time to make the table and chairs this morning, so I used the ones I had on hand.

Before I moved the table into the dining room, I decided to add just a touch of the holidays. So I repainted the room in pinks and stenciled gold stars on the ceiling. Then, while the home-made bread was rising, I took antique candle molds and made the dishes to use for breakfast. These were made from Hungarian clay, which you can get in almost any Hungarian craft store.

Well, I must run. I need to finish the buttonholes on the dress I'm wearing for breakfast. I'll get out the sled and drive this note to the post office as soon as the glue dries on the envelope I'll be making. Hope my breakfast guests don't stay too long. I have forty thousand cranberries to string with bay leaves before my speaking engagement at noon.

Love,

Martha

P.S. When I made the ribbon for this typewriter, I used one-eighth-inch gold gauze. I soaked the gauze in a mixture of white grapes and blackberries that I grew, picked, and crushed last week just for fun.

Dear Martha,

I'm writing this on the back of an old shopping list. Pay no attention to the coffee and jelly stains. I'm twenty minutes late getting my daughter up for school, trying to pack a lunch with one hand while talking on the phone to the dog pound with the other. Seems old Ruff needs bailing out again. Burned my arm on the curling iron when I was trying to make those cute curly fries last night. How *do* they do that?

Still can't find the scissors to cut out some snowflakes. Tried using an old disposable razor—trashed the tablecloth in the process, but at least it no longer has those annoying fuzzballs that caused the water glasses to tip over.

Tried that cranberry-stringing thing, but the frozen cranberries got all mushy when I defrosted them in the microwave. Oh, and here's a tip: Don't use those new chocolate-flavored Rice Krispies in that snowball recipe unless you're ready for some rather disgusting comments from your kids. I put a few too many marshmallows in mine, and they flattened out into disks I thought looked like hockey pucks—but the kids insisted were cow patties.

Gotta go. The smoke alarm is going off.

Love,
Erma

What's a Mother to Do?

KATHY PEEL

Women's roles have changed dramatically over the past thirty years. Before the mid-1960s most young women went to college to find a husband. To them, a bachelor of arts degree was secondary to meeting the right bachelor. They dreamed of marrying Ward Cleaver, driving a wood-panel station wagon, and living happily ever after in suburbia.

By the end of the decade, a new breed of women moved into the dorm. I had the good luck or misfortune (depending on how you look at it) of being part of this changing generation. Bored with the thought of ironing boxer shorts and spending half their days studying meat loaf recipes, women of this era wanted *real* careers and equal partnership with their husbands.

By droves they enrolled in business, premed, and engineering classes—formerly foreign territory to women. The male students welcomed their new classmates with open arms—mainly because bralessness was in vogue.

I noticed that when older sorority sisters returned to campus for homecoming and witnessed this new spirit of freedom, they acted appalled—but were secretly green with envy. When weekend festivities ended, the alumni corralled their screaming preschoolers into sensible family cars and drove back to neighborhoods of tract homes to resume predictable lifestyles.

Curiosity heightened among young suburban mothers as reports trickled back that women were graduating and actually landing jobs in sleek skyscrapers. News of feminine corporate success spread like wildfire at waterless-cookware parties. Many a housewife longed to trade in her station wagon for a subway pass. She dreamed of wearing sophisticated suits and high heels to important meetings. Her days would be spent writing memos, eating business lunches at fine restaurants, and answering only important phone calls.

While moving endless mounds of clothes from the washer to the dryer, she began planning her move to the marketplace—to do something *meaningful* with her life. "Surely there is more to life than measuring fabric softener and playing space patrol," she silently hoped. She didn't have a clue that the world of Wall Street might be a tad overrated. It was hard to tell that the savvy woman on the cover of *Business Monthly* had perspiration circles under the arms of her silk blouse, runs in her high-density support hose, and hemorrhoid cream around her eyes to shrink the bags.

Meanwhile, up on the twenty-seventh floor, a corporate woman's stress-filled world is growing more painful by the hour—and so do her corns. Night after night she works late—only to return home to a dark apartment to eat Noodle Helper alone. "I'd give up my corner office in a minute if I had any prospects of marrying, settling down, and having babies," she says. "What I'd give for the freedom to jump out of bed in the morning after a decent night's rest, give the house a quick once-over, and enjoy the day watching my children play happily together."

Trust me, this woman may be knowledgeable about market trends, but when it comes to understanding motherhood and what it takes to run a household, her mind can be summed up in two words: *altered state*. First, a word about babies: No doubt she thinks postpartum blues are a range of decorator paint colors, stretch marks are lines on the floor of her health club, and colic is a gourmet garlic substitute.

Little does she know a good night's rest is two hours of uninterrupted sleep. Giving the house a quick once-over means clearing a path with a snowplow wired to the front of the vacuum. And expecting to find children playing happily together is like thinking the press will discover Bill Clinton and Rush Limbaugh playing horseshoes after a picnic lunch.

So who's right—the woman who craves a career outside the home in the marketplace or the upwardly mobile professional who longs to spend her days on the home front? Since I'm smarter than I look, I won't pretend to be an outside expert on this issue. And as far as what motherhood means to you, I'm going to leave that up to you. I've learned over the years that arguing with women over an emotionally charged topic— whether to work outside the home, whether to choose private or public schools, etc.—gives me about as much joy as burning my neck with a curling iron. . . .

Now lest you think I'm setting myself up as the model mother or state-of-the-art family manager, please understand I'm far from perfect. Don't look for pat answers on how to stop sibling rivalry, turn your child into a genius, prepare gourmet meals, and pour spiritual values into empty containers. Under oath, my kids will tell you that I've got a long way to go. Just today I took my seven-year-old in for his five-year-old checkup, my sophomore complained his jeans have been in the to-be-washed pile so long that he's outgrown them, and the mayor put our house on his "Clean Up the City" hit list. Xanadu it's not.

I hope as you read this book you will laugh at me and learn to laugh with and at yourself.

Approximately three thousand years ago Solomon wrote in Proverbs 17:22, "A cheerful heart is good medicine" (NIV). And Norman Cousins stated in *Anatomy of an Illness* that joyful laughter causes the brain to create endorphins that relieve stress and activate the immune system. Personally, I can use a dose of this kind of medicine on a regular basis.

—from *The Stomach Virus and Other Forms of Family Bonding*

Once Upon a Time

*O*nce upon a time . . . we were little girls. By day we read from our books of fairy tales, and by night we dreamed of the way our lives would turn out. . . .

Do you ever wonder, *What happened?* Does it seem that somewhere among the prince, the kids, the laundry, and the carpool the fairy-tale company must have been bought out and is now bankrupt? Does it seem that life played a cruel trick on us? Most of us would openly acknowledge that what we ended up with is so very different than our dreams. It's not exactly like we really were Snow White or Cinderella or Sleeping Beauty. But please, shouldn't there be a few recognizable parallels?

This is where the voice of reason reminds us we can't compare our lives to theirs because they were fairy-tale women in very different times. Theirs would be totally different stories if they had to face what we do today. Walt's women wouldn't have it so easy if they had to make it in today's world.

Can't you just see Cinderella on the Stairmaster trying to keep those thighs firm? She's out of breath, talking on her cell phone: "I'll be there as soon as I can, Charming. I have to finish my workout and then stop by the grocery and pick up the flowers for the table. Will the carriage be arriving at six?"

46

What about Sleeping Beauty, propped up in bed on all her pillows, talking anxiously on the phone? "No, Mother, you didn't wake me. I can't sleep. No, I haven't heard from the prince yet, so don't ask me about it. Yes, I'm sure he's still coming."

Or Snow White, sitting in a tangle of computer wires, writing the Christmas letters? "Sleepy is in the second grade now and stays awake through fourth period. We're so proud of him. Grumpy is taking his Ritalin, and it's really helping him."

It would be interesting to watch each of them face some of our struggles and try to stay positive in our over-whelmingly negative world. Let them deal with the reality of the modern world. Too often we can't tell whether what we are doing matters, and our hopeful hearts grow weary and defeated. Nowadays when we watch those fairy tales with our kids and grandkids, we feel more like the wicked stepmother than the woman with the dreams. If we were to ask, "Mirror, Mirror on the wall, who's the fairest of them all?" it would probably answer, "Stop asking me! It's not you, for crying out loud."

I wonder if our legendary three would begin to feel the drain that so many of us feel—as if life has passed us by, and we'll never have our dream life. Would they, too, feel despair lurking around each corner and face the strong temptation to give up? Too tired to keep their hearts from getting cynical, they might start thinking, *What is the use? Why bother? It's all gone wrong anyway. I quit!*

Then we might see that . . .

Cinderella is lying on the couch in her therapist's office. She is complaining and crying loudly, "I know he was a prince when I married him, but he certainly isn't one anymore."

Sleeping Beauty is still in her bedroom, propped up on her pillows and talking on the phone, but this time to the pharmacist. "Yes, this is Sleeping Beauty again. If you could just give me something . . . No, I don't have a prescription. I'm supposed to be asleep!"

Snow White is running full speed through the living room with a frying pan, yelling at the dwarfs, "Close that door! How many times do I have to tell you, we are not air-conditioning the mines?" . . .

The illusion of a sugary sweet world looks perfectly positive, and the darkness of the so-called real world seems honestly negative, so we rationalize that together they will balance each other out. It doesn't work that way. Two halves will never make a whole when both are illusions. We have "fake it" on one side and "get over it" on the other. Pick your poison—saccharin or arsenic; it's death either way. . . .

The woman with a princess heart is no Pollyanna, but she's not the perennial pessimist either. Don't take either fork in the road. Plow straight ahead and through the middle, no matter how uncomfortable it gets. Stay down from the castles in the air. Stay above the dungeons in the dark. And don't forget—you have been recognized. You are loved. And one day, all will be well. The golden truths of the fairy tales will clear the path through the middle of the forest and keep you on the right course toward the invisible kingdom, where all princess hearts are called to live.

—from *Keeping a Princess Heart in a Not-So-Fairy-Tale World*

What Did *You* Do Today?

PHIL CALLOWAY

I have been a husband for nearly ten years now, so needless to say I know virtually everything there is to know about my wife's needs. For instance, I know that she can get by without sleep for three days and three nights—but definitely not without chocolate. I also know that she needs flowers, nurturing, romance, protection, a listening ear, clean laundry, and clothes that fit. Whereas my basic needs are . . . well, pizza.

It is a quarter to five right now, and I'm sitting at my desk thinking about my need for pizza. It's been one of those days at the office. A computer blip swallowed half the morning's work, and nothing went right after that. I had no time for lunch. Deadlines loom. Reports beckon. And my stomach growls. It is saying, "Hey, give us pizza. We need pizza."

As the clock struggles toward 5:00 P.M., however, the growling is muffled in visions of home. Dinner will be store-bought Coke and homemade pizza. Toppings will include large hunks of pepperoni, layers of ham, and enough cheese to blanket Switzerland. The crust will be light, yet crunchy, flavored with a generous pinch of oregano. When I arrive, Ramona will be waiting at the door, her hair permed, her lips pursed. The children will be setting the table, newly washed smiles gracing each face. "Hi, Daddy!" they will say in unison. "We sure missed you."

49

Following dinner, the children will beg to be put to bed early. "We want you and Mom to have some time alone," they will say. "You've probably had a tough day."

As I park the car, however, I realize that something has gone terribly wrong. For one thing, half the neighborhood is in our yard. As I enter the house, I find the other half. They are riffling through our refrigerator. In the kitchen Ramona is bent over the dishwasher, cleaning out the last of the silverware. The table is piled high with laundry, and the stove holds not even a hint of supper.

Several times in my life I have said things people did not appreciate. This is one of those times.

"So what's for supper?" I ask. "Roast beef?"

There is silence.

I sit down beside the laundry and make an even bigger mistake. "So," I say, "what did *you* do today?"

Sometimes my wife moves very quickly. This is one of those times. Ramona stands up straight, brandishing a sharp fork.

"What did *I* do today?"

She walks swiftly across the room—still holding the fork.

"WHAT DID I DO TODAY?"

She hands me a piece of paper. A piece of paper women everywhere should own. Then she stands over me as I read it.

WHAT I DID TODAY

3:21 A.M.—Woke up. Took Jeffrey to the bathroom.

3:31 A.M.—Woke up. Took Jeffrey back to bed.

3:46 A.M.—Got you to quit snoring.

3:49 A.M.—Went to sleep.

5:11 A.M.—Woke up. Took Jeffrey to bathroom.

6:50 A.M.—Alarm went off. Mentally reviewed all I had to do today.

7:00 A.M.—Alarm went off.

7:10 A.M.—Alarm went off. Contemplated doing something violent to alarm clock.

7:19 A.M.—Got up. Got dressed. Made bed. Warned Stephen.

7:20 A.M.—Warned Stephen.

7:21 A.M.—Spanked Stephen. Held Stephen. Prayed with Stephen.

7:29 A.M.—Fed boys a breakfast consisting of Cheerios, orange juice, and something that resembled toast. Scolded Jeffrey for mixing them.

7:35 A.M.—Woke Rachael.

7:38 A.M.—Had devotions.

7:49 A.M.—Made Stephen's lunch. Tried to answer Jeffrey's question, "Why does God need people?" Warned Stephen.

8:01 A.M.—Woke Rachael.

8:02 A.M.—Started laundry.

8:03 A.M.—Took rocks out of washing machine.

8:04 A.M.—Started laundry.

8:13 A.M.—Planned grocery list. Tried to answer Jeffrey's question, "Why do we need God?"

8:29 A.M.—Woke Rachael (third time).

8:30 A.M.—Helped Stephen with homework.

8:31 A.M.—Sent Stephen to school. Told him to remember his lunch.

8:32 A.M.—Had breakfast with Rachael. Porridge.

Rest of morning—Took Stephen's lunch to him. Returned library books. Explained why a cover was missing. Mailed letters. Bought groceries. Shut TV off. Planned birthday party. Cleaned house. Wiped noses. Wiped windows. Wiped bottoms. Shut TV off. Cleaned spaghetti out of carpet. Cut bite marks off the cheese. Made owl-shaped sandwiches.

12:35 P.M.—Put wet clothes in dryer.

12:35 P.M.—Sat down to rest.

12:39 P.M.—Scolded Jeffrey. Helped him put clothes back in dryer.

12:45 P.M.—Agreed to baby-sit for a friend. Cut tree sap out of Rachael's hair. Regretted baby-sitting decision. Killed assorted insects. Read to the kids. Clipped ten fingernails. Sent kids outside. Unpacked groceries. Watered plants. Swept floor. Picked watermelon seeds off linoleum. Read to the kids.

3:43 P.M.—Stephen came home. Warned Stephen.

3:46 P.M.—Put Band-Aids on knees. Organized task force to clean kitchen. Cleaned parts of house. Accepted appointments to local committee (secretary said, "You probably have extra time since you don't work"). Tried to answer Rachael's question, "Why are boys and girls different?" Listened to a zillion more questions. Answered a few. Cleaned out dishwasher. Briefly considered running away from home.

5:21 P.M.—Husband arrived, looking for peace, perfection, and pizza.

I am finished reading now, but Ramona is not through. "Of course, not all my days go this smoothly," she says, still clutching the fork.

"Any questions?"

Often when Ramona and I are at public gatherings, she is asked The Question: "Do you work?" I'm glad she is not holding a fork at this point. Sometimes I wish she'd say, "Actually, I work days, nights, and weekends. How about you?" But she doesn't. She's a kind woman. She practices what I preach. Once, however, she confided that she wishes she had the eloquence to respond as one woman did: "I am socializing three Homo sapiens in the dominant values of the Judeo-Christian tradition in order that they might be instruments for the transformation of the social order into the teleologically prescribed utopia inherent in the eschaton."

Then she would ask, "And what is it you do?"

—from *I Used to Have Answers, Now I Have Kids*

Remember?

ANONYMOUS

When my three-year-old son opened the birthday gift from his grandmother, he discovered a water pistol. He squealed with delight and headed for the nearest sink. I was not so pleased. I turned to Mom and said, "I'm surprised at you. Don't you remember how we used to drive you crazy with water guns?" Mom smiled and then replied, "I remember."

I Was the Perfect Mother
—But I Got Over It

• • • • • • • • • Kathy Peel • • • • • • • • •

I've often wondered why children don't come with a warning label. When we brought our first child home from the hospital, I didn't know I had committed myself for the next twelve months to functioning in a state somewhere between comatose and catatonic. Neither did I realize that I'd signed over my rights to carry on an uninterrupted adult conversation for the next eighteen years.

In the last trimester of my pregnancy, I fantasized about our new family. In my dream I was, of course, the perfect mother. Our home was spotless and smelled of baby lotion. Dressed in a beautiful Pima cotton gown and robe, I rocked our infant who lay quietly bundled in lacy blankets. Every hair on my head was perfectly arranged and my makeup flawless. I had already lost the fifty-five pounds I managed to gain in eight months. And Bill stood by my side, hand-feeding me grapes and gourmet crackers.

Talk about rude awakenings. First of all, the aroma that permeated our house gave new meaning to the word *asphyxiation.* I wondered why baby stores don't sell gas masks. And after twenty-four hours of nonstop infant discharge from both ends, I didn't own a clean item of clothing. Surely I could sell the research rights to the stains I couldn't identify. Why didn't disposable diaper ads show parents dodging projectile diarrhea? As for my hair and makeup, my new look protected me from all door-to-door salesmen. They ran when I answered the door. And Bill told me not to worry about the fifty-five pounds. He was sure I still had time to qualify for the trained whale show. (He was just trying to kid me out of the doldrums, but I didn't think it was a laughing matter.)

It took about a week for us to throw out any preconceived philosophies we once held about family life. Our home was out of control. But I'm a proud person, and I wanted the outside world to think that universities were funding programs to study our astute parenting skills. Early on we tried to impress our friends with our shrewd tactics.

I announced one night at a dinner party that Bill and I had made an important decision: Not a drop of anything foreign would touch our child's lips—I planned to nurse for three years. It only took eight months and two jars of nipple balm to figure out that teething babies aren't exactly user-friendly.

As our firstborn grew up, we continued to use a trial-and-error method—mostly error—to formulate our parenting strategy. High on our list of priorities we listed good nutrition, believing that a healthy family is a happy family—which may be true in some cases. (It had the opposite effect on ours.)

I got into this nutritional thing in a big way. I decided with fervor, "Not a granule of white sugar or refined flour will pass our threshold again." I drove to a farm to buy honey straight from the hive, bought undefiled peanut butter for fifteen dollars a jar, stocked up on organic rice cakes, and baked homemade bread—which we could have used for a doorstop.

Every morning I self-righteously prepared a healthy lunch for my first grader. I turned up my nose at less conscientious mothers who actually put chips and cupcakes in their children's lunches. How irresponsible! I thought smugly.

When it came time for my parent-teacher conference, the teacher assured me that John was doing very well in school. But she questioned my attitude toward nutrition. "Did you know, Mrs. Peel, that your son eats doughnuts and candy bars every day for lunch?" It seems that by noon, John's sandwich had turned into a ball of mush. And the kids used my cookies for Frisbees on the playground. The other children felt sorry for John, so they took turns donating their extras to him every day. The Rice Cake Era of our family ended—suddenly. And, to tell the truth, I was relieved. I'm still not a very good cook. And, while we try to limit sweets and junk foods, I realized that I'd gone overboard—when it was really my bread that should have. It would have made the perfect anchor.

—from *Do Plastic Surgeons Take Visa?
and Other Confessions of a Desperate Woman*

The Mom Test

• • • • • • • • • • • ANONYMOUS • • • • • • • • • •

You know you're a mom when . . .

- You count the sprinkles on each kid's cupcake to make sure they're equal.
- You want to take out a contract on the kid who broke your child's favorite toy and made him or her cry.
- You have time to shave only one leg at a time.
- You hide in the bathroom to be alone.
- Your child throws up, and you catch it.
- Someone else's kid throws up at a party, and you keep eating.
- You consider finger paint to be a controlled substance.
- You dream that frozen pizzas are on sale and wake up you're so happy.
- The material possession you want most in life is a minivan.
- You've mastered the art of placing large quantities of foods on a plate without anything touching.
- Your child insists that you read *Once upon a Potty* out loud in the lobby of the doctor's office, or, better yet, in the lobby of Grand Central Station, and you do it.

- You hire a sitter because you haven't been out with your husband in ages, then spend half the night talking about and checking on the kids.

- You hope ketchup is a vegetable because it's the only one your child eats.

- You cling to the high moral ground on toy weapons, while your child chews his toast into the shape of a gun.

- You can't bear the thought of your son's first girlfriend.

- You can't bear the thought of his wife even more.

- You donate to charities in the hope that your child won't get that disease.

- You find yourself cutting your husband's sandwiches into unusual shapes.

- You fast-forward through the scene when the hunter shoots Bambi's mother.

- You use your own saliva to clean your child's face.

- You obsess when your child clings to you on his first day of school, then obsess when he skips in without looking back on his second day.

- You can't bear to give away baby clothes—it's so final.

- You hear your mother's voice coming out of your mouth when you say, "Not in your good clothes!"

- You stop criticizing the way your mother raised you.

- You read that the average five-year-old asks 437 questions a day and feel proud that your kid is above average.

- You think at least once a day, *I'm not cut out for this job,* but you know you wouldn't trade it for anything in the world.

Are You Ready for Motherhood?

· · · · · · · BARBARA JOHNSON · · · · · · ·

Now, if you're wondering whether you have what it takes to be a *mommy,* here's a list of preparations to help you get ready for the blessed event:

Mother's Preparation for Pregnancy: From the food co-op, obtain a twenty-five-pound bag of pinto beans and attach it to your waist with a belt. Wear it everywhere you go for nine months. Then remove ten of the beans to indicate the baby has been born.

Financial Preparation: Arrange for direct deposit of your family's paycheck to be split equally between the nearest grocery store and the pediatrician's office for the next two decades.

Mess-Management Preparation: Smear grape jelly on the living room furniture and curtains. Now plunge your hands into a bag of potting soil, wipe them on the walls, and highlight the smudges with Magic Markers.

Inhalation Therapy Preparation: Empty a carton of milk onto the cloth upholstery of the family car, park the vehicle in a sunny spot, and then leave it to ripen for the month of August. Rub a half-finished lollipop through your hair, then hide it in the glove compartment.

Pain-Endurance Preparation: Collect enough small, plastic, superhero action figures to fill a fifty-five-gallon drum. (You may substitute thumbtacks.) Ask a friend to spread them all over the floor of your house after you've gone to bed, paying special attention to the stairway. Set your alarm for 2 A.M., and when it goes off, rush madly around the darkened house, trying to remember where you left the cordless phone (or the baby).

Shopping Preparation: Herd a flock of goats through the grocery store. Always keep every goat in sight and bring enough money to pay for whatever they eat or destroy.

Aerobic-Agility Preparation: Try to dress the family cat in a small pantsuit, complete with button shirt, snap-leg pants, lace-up shoes, and a bowtie while the neighbor's German shepherd barks out his encouragement from two feet away. (Make sure medics are standing by.)

Mealtime Preparation: Sit at the kitchen counter and carefully spoon strained peas and chocolate pudding into a plastic bag. When the bag is completely full, tie a knot to close it, place it on the kitchen counter at eye level about a foot from your face, then ask your spouse to smash the bag with a dictionary.

Attitude Preparation: Have a schoolteacher friend record the sounds of her second-graders scratching their fingernails across a chalkboard. Then fill a small canvas bag with ten pounds of cat litter, soak it thoroughly in water, attach the bag to a tape player with large speakers, and insert the nails-on-chalkboard recording. Beginning at 8 P.M., pick up the bag and hold it against your shoulder, play the chalkboard recording at its loudest volume, and waltz around the room with a bumping-and-swooping step. Continue for forty minutes, then gently lay down the bag and turn off the tape player. Repeat hourly until 5 A.M. then crawl in bed, set the alarm for 6 A.M., get up and make breakfast while looking cheerful. Repeat for the next five years.

The funny thing about these silly preparations is that somehow all of us parents pass it when we have to. (Well, maybe not the part about looking cheerful while cooking breakfast, but the rest of it, we usually muddle through.) If you're in the middle of the "testing" period right now, remember that you're enrolled in a course that's been a perpetual requirement since Adam and Eve. You *will* get through it (unless, of course, you end up weaving doilies in the home for the bewildered first!). And *someday* you'll be rewarded.

—from *Leaking Laffs Between Pampers and Depends*

The Matchmaker

JANE AUSTEN

I t is a truth universally acknowledged, that a single man in possession of a good fortune must be in want of a wife.

However little known the feelings or views of such a man may be on his first entering a neighborhood, this truth is so well fixed in the minds of the surrounding families, that he is considered as the rightful property of some one or other of their daughters.

"My dear Mr. Bennet," said his lady to him one day, "have you heard that Netherfield Park is let at last?"

Mr. Bennet replied that he had not.

"But it is," returned she, "for Mrs. Long has just been here, and she told me all about it."

Mr. Bennet made no answer.

"Do not you want to know who has taken it?" cried his wife impatiently.

"You want to tell me, and I have no objection to hearing it."

This was invitation enough.

"Why, my dear, you must know, Mrs. Long says that Netherfield is taken by a young man of large fortune from the north of England; that he came down on Monday in a chaise and four to see the place, and was so much delighted with it that he agreed with Mr. Morris immediately; that he is to take possession before Michaelmas, and some of his servants are to be in the house by the end of next week."

"What is his name?"

"Bingley."

"Is he married or single?"

"Oh! single, my dear, to be sure! A single man of large fortune; four or five thousand a year. What a fine thing for our girls!"

"How so? How can it affect them?"

"My dear Mr. Bennet," replied his wife, "how can you be so tiresome! You must know that I am thinking of his marrying one of them."

"Is that his design in settling here?"

"Design! Nonsense, how can you talk so! But it is very likely that he may fall in love with one of them, and therefore you must visit him as soon as he comes."

"I see no occasion for that. You and the girls may go, or you may send them by themselves, which perhaps will be still better; for, as you are as handsome as any of them, Mr. Bingley might like you the best of the party."

"My dear, you flatter me. I certainly have had my share of beauty, but I do not pretend to be any thing extraordinary now. When a woman has five grown-up daughters, she ought to give over thinking of her own beauty."

"In such cases, a woman has not often much beauty to think of."

"But, my dear, you must indeed go and see Mr. Bingley when he comes into the neighborhood."

"It is more than I engage for, I assure you."

"But consider your daughters. Only think what an establishment it would be for one of them. Sir William and Lady Lucas are determined to go, merely on that account, for in general, you know they visit no newcomers. Indeed you must go, for it will be impossible for us to visit him, if you do not."

"You are over-scrupulous, surely. I dare say Mr. Bingley will be very glad to see you; and I will send a few lines by you to assure him of my hearty consent to his marrying whichever he chooses of the girls; though I must throw in a good word for my little Lizzy."

"I desire you will do no such thing. Lizzy is not a bit better than the others; and I am sure she is not half so handsome as Jane, nor half so good humored as Lydia. But you are always giving her the preference."

"They have none of them much to recommend them," replied he. "They are all silly and ignorant like other girls; but Lizzy has something more of quickness than her sisters."

"Mr. Bennet, how can you abuse your own children in such a way? You take delight in vexing me. You have no compassion on my poor nerves."

"You mistake me, my dear. I have a high respect for your nerves. They are my old friends. I have heard you mention them with consideration these twenty years at least."

"Ah! you do not know what I suffer."

"But I hope you will get over it, and live to see many young men of four thousand a year come into the neighborhood."

"It will be no use to us if twenty such should come, since you will not visit them."

"Depend upon it, my dear, that when there are twenty I will visit them all."

Mr. Bennet was so odd a mixture of quick parts, sarcastic humor, reserve, and caprice, that the experience of three and twenty years had been insufficient to make his wife understand his character. Her mind was less difficult to develop. She was a woman of mean understanding, little information, and uncertain temper. When she was discontented, she fancied herself nervous. The business of her life was to get her daughters married. . . .

—from *Pride and Prejudice*

My Mommy

• • • • • • • • • ANONYMOUS • • • • • • • • •

One summer evening during a violent thunderstorm, a mother was tucking her little boy into bed. After reading a bedtime story, she said prayers with him. Then she got up and was about to turn off the light when he asked with a tremor in his voice, "Mommy, will you sleep with me tonight?"

The mother smiled and gave him a reassuring hug. "I can't, honey," she said. "I have to sleep in Daddy's room with him."

A long silence was broken at last by her little boy's shaky, small voice: "The big sissy."

Who Am I?

NICOLE JOHNSON

After putting her children to bed, a mother changed into old slacks and a droopy blouse, took off her makeup, and proceeded to wash her hair. As she heard the children getting more and more rambunctious, her patience grew thin. At last she threw a towel around her head and stormed into their room, putting them back to bed with stern warnings. As she left the room, she heard her three-year-old say with a trembling voice, "Who was that?"

I wonder the same thing about myself! Between dress-up evenings, afternoon runs to the grocery store in sweats, and stay-in-my-pajamas-and-work mornings, I stay in wardrobe confusion. From changing diapers to exchanging business cards to rearranging furniture, the tasks that we perform during the day are no help in determining who we are. We can do anything, but that doesn't mean we want it to define us. Bringing home the bacon, frying it up in the pan, changing a flat on the way home, starting to feel like I'm a man! But I'm a woooman. No wonder we are confused about who we are. . . .

Who am I? Have you ever lain awake at night asking this question? I take that back. Most women work too hard to miss sleep by lying awake at night, much less asking questions! So the questions probably come at other times. *Who am I?* Do you ever feel that you're faking your life? That you're living someone else's life, and you're not sure whose? You wonder how you got to this place of disguise. You want to give yourself to God, but what self are you going to give?

Your work life? What you do doesn't determine who you are. Your beauty? What you wear or the hairstyle you sport, or how much makeup you have on isn't necessarily the "real you." Your relationships? All your roles as wife, mother, and friend are not the sum total of your identity. So what do we give and who are we?

The answer is (D), all of the above.

We are like onions. We can't merely peel away all the layers, because they are us, as long as they are true to the core. You don't get to the middle of an onion and find an apple core. The onion begins at the core, and each and every layer builds upon the "onion-ness" inside. An authentic life and self is one in which the layers on the outside are merely expressions of the core on the inside.

—from *Fresh-Brewed Life*

For Laughs . . .

The following are actual classified ads that have been placed in newspapers.

Classified Ads

- ❀ "German Shepherd. Eighty-five pounds. Neutered. Speaks German. Free."

- ❀ "Free ducks. You catch."

- ❀ "Snow blower for sale . . . only used on snowy days."

- ❀ "Shakespeare's Pizza. Free chopsticks."

- ❀ "Georgia peaches, California grown—eighty-nine cents per pound."

- ❀ "Vacation special: Have your home exterminated."

- ❀ "Get rid of aunts: Zap does the job in twenty-four hours."

- ❀ "Carpal Tunnel Syndrome—free sample!"

- ❀ "Toaster: A gift that every member of the family appreciates. Automatically burns toast."

- ❀ "Wanted: Haircutter. Excellent growth potential."

❀ "Dinner special: turkey $2.35; chicken or beef $2.25; children $2.00."

❀ "His and hers bicycles: $25 each or both for $55."

❀ "We'll move you worldwide throughout the country."

❀ "We do not tear your clothing with machinery. We do it carefully by hand."

❀ "Dog for sale: eats anything and is fond of children."

❀ "Stock up and save. Limit: one."

❀ "Wanted to buy: fishing net; must have no holes."

❀ "To let: Four-bedroom house close to town. No poets."

❀ "Used cars: Why go elsewhere to be cheated? Come here first!"

❀ "Three-year-old teacher need for preschool. Experience preferred."

❀ "Auto Repair Service. Free pick-up and delivery. Try us once; you'll never go anywhere again."

❀ "Illiterate? Write today for free help."

❀ "Semi-annual after-Christmas sale."

Part III

Whistle While You Work

Laughter Is the Spice of Everyday Life

The most wasted of all days is one without laughter.

—E. E. CUMMINGS

Everything is funny as long as it is happening to someone else.

—WILL ROGERS

Humor involves a sense of proportion and a power of seeing yourself from the outside.

—C. S. LEWIS

Balancing the Nine to Fives

• • • • • • • • • LUCI SWINDOLL • • • • • • • • •

Thus far, the topics we have considered in terms of celebration have been enjoyable pursuits—savoring the moment, delighting in birthdays, mealtimes, and reunions, reveling in fellowship with our friends and families, and even relishing the joys of learning—both in formal education and just for the fun of it. All of these have been somewhat instinctive in our desire to celebrate because they follow the natural course of what gratifies us without a lot of effort. However, when we come to the idea of celebrating work, that's another story. Or, at least that's the tale most of us have been taught. We've grown to believe these clichés:

- Watch out for ambition! It can get you into a lot of hard work.
- The thing most of us don't like about work is that it's so daily.
- Work is the annoyance people have to endure between coffee breaks.
- The trouble with getting to work on time is that it makes the day so long.
- Never buy anything with a handle on it. It might mean work!

I saw a good one several months ago when I was standing at a public counter in a nearby city hall. It was typed on a small card and taped to the wall:

```
If you don't believe in
the  resurrection  of  the
dead,  stick  around  here
till 5 P.M.
```

Many of us embrace the idea that work is an affliction, a drudgery, a crushing burden against society that deforms us and holds us back from being all we could be if we just didn't have to report to a job. If labor were reduced (or preferably, eliminated altogether), life would be richer and sweeter. This seems to be the outlook of the majority. At least that has been my discovery as I have chatted with people almost everywhere I've traveled. To most, work is a drag!

There also exists the extreme opposite viewpoint: Work is not a curse; it is humanity's greatest blessing. Were it not for the virtue of work, all our idleness would be wasted or misspent in such a fashion that we would be in constant trouble or mischief. If a person doesn't work, he or she becomes slovenly in habits, behavior, and appearance. The people who think this way live by these homilies:

- It's simply fantastic the amount of work you can get done if you don't do anything else.

- The workman has to perform for his subsistence night and day.

- You can often gauge a man's ambition by whether he hates his alarm clock or considers it his dear friend.

- If you think you work harder than the average worker, you're an average worker.

My question is, Why can't there be a happy medium? Surely there is an enjoyable way of accomplishing the tasks before us whether that's in an office, in a store, in sports, or in school. Wherever we find ourselves employed, whenever we have a job to do, uniform principles should apply that create a balanced life. Our job should be one where our labor produces dignity, self-respect, and an attitude of happy diligence. We need to stop looking at work as simply a means of earning a living and start realizing it is one of the elemental ingredients of making a life! I like the words of Aristotle:

Amusement is needed more amid serious occupations than at other times, for he who is hard at work has need for relaxation, and amusement gives relaxation.

—from *You Bring the Confetti, God Brings the Joy*

Hymns for All Callings

• • • • • • • • • ANONYMOUS • • • • • • • • •

The airline captain's hymn: "Jesus, Savior, Pilot Me"
The baker's hymn: "I Need Thee Every Hour"
The dentist's hymn: "Crown Him with Many Crowns"
The contractor's hymn: "The Church's One Foundation"
The boxer's hymn: "Fight the Good Fight"
The politician's hymn: "Standing on the Promises"
The IRS's hymn: "All to Thee"
The dieter's hymn: "And Can It Be That I Should Gain?"
The electrician's hymn: "Send the Light"
The UFO's hymn: "Come, O Thou Traveler Unknown"
The gossip's hymn: "O for a Thousand Tongues"
The telephone operator's hymn: "We've a Story to Tell to the Nations"

And whatever you do, do it heartily, as to the Lord and not to men.
(Colossians 3:23)

To the Poorhouse with a Smile

• • • • • • • • • BILL COSBY • • • • • • • • •

Because you are feeding both the child and the floor, raising this child will be expensive. The Lord was wise enough to make a woman's pregnancy last nine months. If it were shorter, people with temporary insanity might have two or three kids a year, and they would be wiped out before the first one had learned to talk. You know why John D. Rockefeller had all that money? Because he had only one child, so he didn't have to spend ninety thousand dollars on Snoopy pens and Superhero mugs and Smurf pajamas and Barbie Ferraris.

It doesn't make any difference how much money a father earns, his name is always Dad-Can-I; and he always wonders whether these little people were born to beg. I bought each of my five children everything up to a Rainbow Brite jacuzzi and still I kept hearing "Dad, can I get . . . Dad, can I go . . . Dad, can I buy . . ."

Like all other children, my five have one great talent: they are gifted beggars. Not one of them ever ran into the room, looked up at me, and said, "I'm really happy that you're my father, and as a tangible token of my appreciation, here's a dollar." If one of them had ever done this, I would have taken his temperature.

A parent quickly learns that no matter how much money you have, you will never be able to buy your kids everything they want. You can take a second mortgage on your house and buy what you think is the entire Snoopy line: Snoopy pajamas, Snoopy under-pants, Snoopy linen, Snoopy shoelaces, Snoopy cologne, and Snoopy soap, but you will never have it all. And if Snoopy doesn't send you to the poorhouse, Calvin Klein will direct the trip. Calvin is the slick operator who sells your kids things for eighty-five dollars that cost seven at Sears. He has created millions of tiny snobs, chil-dren who look disdainfully at you and say, "Nothing from Sears." However, Dad-Can-I fought back: I got some Calvin Klein labels and sewed them into Sears undershorts for my high-fashion junkies.

Sometimes, at three or four in the morning, I open the door to one of the children's bedrooms and watch the light softly fall across their little faces. And then I quietly kneel beside one of the beds and just look at the girl lying there because she is so beauti-ful. And because she is not begging. Kneeling there, I listen rev-erently to the sounds of her breathing.

And then she wakes up and says, "Dad, can I . . ."

—from *Fatherhood*

Excuse Letters

• • • • • • • • • • • ANONYMOUS • • • • • • • • • • •

The routine is familiar: when a student is late or absent from school, a letter from the parents must be supplied for the absence to be excused. Sometimes such letters suggest that the parents were excused from school one too many times in their own youth.

- "My son is under a doctor's care and should not take P.E. today. Please execute him."
- "Please excuse Lisa for being absent. She was sick, and I had her shot."
- "Dear School: Please excuse John being absent on Jan. 28th, 29th, 30th, 31st, 32nd, and also 33rd."
- "Please excuse Gloria from Jim today. She is administrating."
- "Please excuse Roland from P.E. for a few days. Yesterday he fell out of a tree and misplaced his hip."
- "John has been absent because he had two teeth taken out of his face."
- "Carlos was absent yesterday because he was playing football. He was hurt in the growing part."
- "Megan could not come to school today because she has been bothered by very close veins."

- "Please excuse Ray Friday from school. He has very loose vowels."

- "Please excuse Tommy for being absent yesterday. He had diarrhea, and his boots leak."

- "Irving was absent yesterday because he missed his bust."

- "Please excuse Jimmy for being. It was his father's fault."

- "Please excuse Jennifer for missing school yesterday. We forgot to get the Sunday paper off the porch, and when we found it Monday, we thought it was Sunday."

- "Sally won't be in school a week from Friday. We have to attend her funeral."

- "My daughter was absent yesterday because she was tired. She spent a weekend with the Marines."

- "Please excuse Jason for being absent yesterday. He had a cold and could not breed well."

The Party

• • • • • • • Louisa May Alcott • • • • • • • •

Jo! Jo! Where are you?" cried Meg at the foot of the garret stairs.

"Here!" answered a husky voice from above and, running up, Meg found her sister eating apples and crying over *The Heir of Redclyffe*, wrapped up in a comforter on an old three-legged sofa by the sunny window. This was Jo's favorite refuge, and here she loved to retire with half a dozen russets and a nice book, to enjoy the quiet and the society of a pet rat who lived near by and didn't mind her a particle. As Meg appeared, Scrabble whisked into his hole. Jo shook the tears off her cheeks and waited to hear the news.

"Such fun! Only see! A regular note of invitation from Mrs. Gardiner for tomorrow night!" cried Meg, waving the precious paper and then proceeding to read it with girlish delight.

" 'Mrs. Gardiner would be happy to see Miss March and Miss Josephine at a little dance on New Year's Eve.' Marmee is willing we should go, now what shall we wear?"

"What's the use of asking that, when you know we shall wear our poplins, because we haven't got anything else?" answered Jo with her mouth full.

"If I only had a silk!" sighed Meg. "Mother says I may when I'm eighteen perhaps, but two years is an everlasting time to wait."

"I'm sure our pops look like silk, and they are nice enough for us. Yours is as good as new, but I forgot the burn and the tear in mine. Whatever shall I do? The burn shows badly, and I can't take any out."

"You must sit still all you can and keep your back out of sight. The front is all right. I shall have a new ribbon for my hair, and Marmee will lend me her little pearl pin, and my new slippers are lovely, and my gloves will do, though they aren't as nice as I'd like."

"Mine are spoiled with lemonade, and I can't get any new ones, so I shall have to go without," said Jo, who never troubled herself much about dress.

"You must have gloves, or I won't go," cried Meg decidedly. "Gloves are more important than anything else. You can't dance without them, and if you don't I should be so mortified."

"Then I'll stay still. I don't care much for company dancing. It's no fun to go sailing round. I like to fly about and cut capers."

"You can't ask Mother for new ones, they are so expensive, and you are so careless. She said when you spoiled the others that she shouldn't get you any more this winter. Can't you make them do?"

"I can hold them crumpled up in my hand, so no one will know how stained they are. That's all I can do. No! I'll tell you how we can manage, each wear one good one and carry a bad one. Don't you see?"

"Your hands are bigger than mine, and you will stretch my glove dreadfully," began Meg, whose gloves were a tender point with her.

"Then I'll go without. I don't care what people say!" cried Jo, taking up her book.

"You may have it, you may! Only don't stain it, and do behave nicely. Don't put your hands behind you, or stare, or say 'Christopher Columbus!' will you?"

"Don't worry about me. I'll be as prim and proper as I can and not get into any scrapes, if I can help it. Now go and answer your note, and let me finish this splendid story."

So Meg went away to "accept with thanks," look over her dress, and sing blithely as she did up her one real lace frill, while Jo finished her story, her four apples, and had a game of romps with Scrabble.

On New Year's Eve the parlor was deserted, for the two younger girls played dressing maids and the two elder were absorbed in the all-important business of "getting ready for the party." Simple as the toilets were, there was a great deal of running up and down, laughing and talking, and at one time a strong smell of burned hair pervaded the house. Meg wanted a few curls about her face, and Jo undertook to pinch the papered locks with a pair of hot tongs.

"Ought they to smoke like that?" asked Beth from her perch on the bed.

"It's the dampness drying," replied Jo.

"What a queer smell! It's like burned feathers," observed Amy, smoothing her own pretty curls with a superior air.

"There, now I'll take off the papers and you'll see a cloud of little ringlets," said Jo, putting down the tongs. She did take off the papers, but no cloud of ringlets appeared, for the hair came with the papers, and the horrified hairdresser laid a row of little scorched bundles on the bureau before her victim.

"Oh, oh, oh! What have you done? I'm spoiled! I can't go! My hair, oh, my hair!" wailed Meg, looking with despair at the uneven frizzle on her forehead.

"Just my luck! You shouldn't have asked me to do it. I always spoil everything. I'm so sorry, but the tongs were too hot, and so I've made a mess," groaned poor Jo, regarding the little black pancakes with tears of regret.

"It isn't spoiled. Just frizzle it, and tie your ribbon so the ends come on your forehead a bit, and it will look like the last fashion. I've seen many girls do it so," said Amy consolingly.

"Serves me right for trying to be fine. I wish I'd let my hair alone," cried Meg petulantly.

"So do I, it was so smooth and pretty. But it will soon grow out again," said Beth, coming to kiss and comfort the shorn sheep.

After various lesser mishaps, Meg was finished at last, and by the united exertions of the entire family Jo's hair was got up and her dress on. They looked very well in their simple suits, Meg's in silvery drab, with a blue velvet snood, lace frills, and the pearl pin. Jo in maroon, with a stiff, gentlemanly linen collar, and a white chrysanthemum or two for her only ornament. Each put on one nice light glove, and carried one soiled one, and all pronounced the effect "quite easy and fine." Meg's high-heeled slippers were very tight and hurt her, though she would not own it, and Jo's nineteen hairpins all seemed stuck straight into her head, which was not exactly comfortable, but, dear me, let us be elegant or die.

"Have a good time, dearies!" said Mrs. March, as the sisters went daintily down the walk. "Don't eat much supper, and come away at eleven when I send Hannah for you." As the gate clashed behind them, a voice cried from a window . . .

"Girls, girls! Have you both got nice pocket handkerchiefs?"

"Yes, yes, spandy nice, and Meg has cologne on hers," cried Jo, adding with a laugh as they went on, "I do believe Marmee would ask that if we were all running away from an earthquake.

"It is one of her aristocratic tastes, and quite proper, for a real lady is always known by neat boots, gloves, and handkerchief," replied Meg, who had a good many little "aristocratic tastes" of her own.

"Now don't forget to keep the bad breadth out of sight, Jo. Is my sash right? And does my hair look very bad?" said Meg, as she turned from the glass in Mrs. Gardiner's dressing room after a prolonged prink.

"I know I shall forget. If you see me doing anything wrong, just remind me by a wink, will you?" returned Jo, giving her collar a twitch and her head a hasty brush.

"No, winking isn't ladylike. I'll lift my eyebrows if anything is wrong, and nod if you are all right. Now hold your shoulder straight, and take short steps, and don't shake hands if you are introduced to anyone. It isn't the thing."

"How do you learn all the proper ways? I never can. Isn't that music gay?"

Down they went, feeling a trifle timid, for they seldom went to parties, and informal as this little gathering was, it was an event to them.

With many thanks, they said good night and crept in, hoping to disturb no one, but the instant their door creaked, two little nightcaps bobbed up, and two sleepy but eager voices cried out . . .

"Tell about the party! Tell about the party!"

With what Meg called "a great want of manners" Jo had saved some bonbons for the little girls, and they soon subsided, after hearing the most thrilling events of the evening.

"I declare, it really seems like being a fine young lady, to come home from the party in a carriage and sit in my dressing gown with a maid to wait on me," said Meg, as Jo bound up her foot with arnica and brushed her hair.

"I don't believe fine young ladies enjoy themselves a bit more than we do, in spite of our burned hair, old gowns, one glove apiece and tight slippers that sprain our ankles when we are silly enough to wear them."

And I think Jo was quite right.

—from *Little Women*

The More the Merrier

• • • • • • FRANK B. GILBRETH, JR. • • • • • • •

AND ERNESTINE GILBRETH CAREY

Some people used to say that Dad had so many children he couldn't keep track of them. Dad himself used to tell a story about one time when Mother went off to fill a lecture engagement and left him in charge at home. When Mother returned, she asked him if everything had run smoothly.

"Didn't have any trouble except with that one over there," he replied. "But a spanking brought him into line."

Mother could handle any crisis without losing her composure. "That's not one of ours, dear," she said. "He belongs next door."

—from *Cheaper by the Dozen*

"Now What?"

• • • • • • • • • • THELMA WELLS • • • • • • • • •

Ask and it will be given to you; seek and you will find;
knock and the door will be opened to you. (Matthew 7:7 NIV)

My four little granddaughters stayed overnight last Friday and all day Saturday. Little girls ages six, five, four, and two. (Am I crazy or stupid or what?) These wild women in the making took me on as many adventures in that short length of time as I've had all year. Their minds are working in overdrive all the time, and there are absolutely no limits to what they will try.

Our time together started with questions. Grammy, can we dance tonight? Grammy, what are we going to have to eat tonight? Grammy, can we watch a movie tonight? Grammy, who else is coming over tonight? Grammy, have you seen my new dance routine? Grammy, where were you when I called you last week? Grammy, are you going to be in town for my birthday? The barrage of questions was only the beginning. Not only did my little live wires not run out of questions, they did not run out of adventures that kept their attention, even if it was for just a few minutes.

They turned flips and did cartwheels on my bed until my head was spinning. (Papa was in another part of the house, thank God.) They rolled marbles across the floor, on the table, and under the furniture until I made them find every one of the shiny orbs and put them back in the vase of flowers from which they were confiscated. They built a mountain with chairs and plastic pieces of their picnic table, then imagined that a volcano was erupting and they were running for their lives. When I called out their names, as they instructed me to do, the volcano stopped erupting. They wrapped my large, warm, colorful lap blankets around them like evening dresses and pretended that they were going to a formal affair or were beauty queens in a pageant. They tried on all my fur hats, boas, high-heeled shoes, gloves, and other gaudy jewelry and made themselves look their Sunday best.

In the midst of all their imaginative and creative writing, drawing, dressing, and oratory, they inadvertently nearly destroyed the tidiness of my bedroom, their bedroom, my office, and my kitchen by spilling stuff, dropping stuff on the floor, and stringing their belongings from one end of the house to the other.

Does it sound like I'm complaining? Absolutely NOT! I'm simply pointing out that children are on an adventure minute by minute, day by day. We adults can learn something from them.

Their natural curiosity prompts them to ask a lot of questions. I've heard that the only dumb question is the one not asked. So why do adults ask so few questions? Perhaps we think everybody expects us to have all the answers, and we don't. So we stop asking questions, we stop learning and experimenting, and we short-circuit our own experience of adventure.

Most children are not concerned about how tidy things are around them. They love to try new things, stop in the middle, leave the pile of whatever they're playing with, and move on to whatever catches their eye and imagination next. They're constantly on the move. When we get older, we tend to get too caught up in keeping our lives and circumstances tidy; we stop having enough flexibility in our routine to stop and follow wherever our imagination leads. And as a result, we usually stop having fun. Who made up that dumb grown-up rule?

When I've allowed myself to just forget about routine and doing things in the usual ways, my mind seems to open up to fresh and innovative ideas. Adventures I would have missed if I'd kept things in order pop up in front of me like a jack-in-the-box. How fun!

I guess the clincher for my granddaughters was when they were relaxing in the bathtub. (The earlier dancing was part of the "wear them out so they can sleep" strategy.) After they finished splashing the water and chasing the bubbles, they asked enthusiastically, "Grammy, what are we going to do now?" They'd played, messed up, fed their faces, exercised their minds and bodies, even screamed at, hit, and mildly abused each other in their childlike way—and had run Grammy a little loony. *Now what?* Surely there has to be more to do than sleep! They never considered just calling it a day. Their curiosity about what new adventure might be awaiting them was limitless.

I can't count the number of times recently that women who were once real go-getters—intelligent, creative, and energetic—have said to me that they are just tired of life. They are bored with the humdrum of their daily routines and relationships. They see no way out.

I have two words for that kind of thinking. As the kids in my neighborhood would say, "Chill out." You sound like you're overburdened, brain-dead, and on life support in your mind. What you need is a shock wave to jolt your natural curiosity so you can go see what's off the beaten track.

Do you remember those "dumb" questions I mentioned? Start

asking them of yourself and those you respect. Start replacing the self-defeating tapes in your head with statements like, "I can." "I will." "I have a bright future." "I love life and the people in it." Jolt yourself out of your mental ruts by using the magical tool of *wonder.* "I wonder what I'm missing that I've been too busy to investigate." "I wonder how I could look at my situation in a new light." "I wonder what's over there—just around the next bend, off the beaten track. I think I'll go find out!"

Draw yourself a hot bubble bath tonight and splash around for a while. Thoroughly enjoy the moment. Then, with childlike anticipation, ask your heavenly Father, "Now what?" The answer might be, "Get yourself to bed, woman! You're whipped!" Or it might be something totally outside your routine, like "Go ye into the kitchen at midnight and create for thyself a sundae with every kind of dollop and sprinkle ye can find."

Take it from my granddaughters: You never know what you might be missing if you grow up too much and stop asking, "Now what?"

—from *The Great Adventure*

Little Ones

● ● ● ● ● ● ● ● ● ● ● ● Anonymous ● ● ● ● ● ● ● ● ● ●

A child is a curly, dimpled lunatic.

—Ralph Waldo Emerson

On the way to preschool, a doctor had left her stethoscope on the car seat. Her little boy picked it up and began playing with it. *Be still, my heart,* thought the doctor, *my son wants to follow in my footsteps!*

Then the child spoke into the instrument: "Welcome to McDonald's. May I take your order?"

When I called home one day, my six-year-old son answered the phone. "Hello," he said, panting a little. I said, "Hi, Nick. Wow, you sound out of breath." He replied, "No, I have more."

A father was reading Bible stories to his young son. He read, "The man named Lot was warned to take his wife and flee out of the city, but his wife looked back and was turned to salt." His son then asked, "What happened to the flea?"

I told my boys, aged nine and six, that I wanted to stop and get some hair coloring. My six year old asked what color I was getting and why. I told him that it was just to cover my gray and left it at that. They were like kids in a candy store, searching for the "perfect" color. We agreed on one, bought it, and left. That weekend, at church, a lady said she really liked the color of my hair. My nine-year-old beamed and said, "Thanks, I picked it out!"

A little boy was in a relative's wedding. As he was coming down the aisle he would take two steps, stop, and turn to the crowd (alternating between bride's side and groom's side), put his hands up like claws, and roar. Step, step, *Roar*, step step, *Roar*, all the way down the aisle. The crowd was near tears from laughing so hard by the time he reached the pulpit. The little boy, however, was getting more and more distressed from all the laughing and was almost crying by the time he reached the pulpit. When asked what he was doing, the child sniffed and said, "I was being the Ring Bear."

A woman was at the beach with her children when her four-year-old son ran up to her, grabbed her hand, and led her to the shore, where a sea gull lay dead in the sand.

"Mommy, what happened to him?" he asked.

"He died and went to Heaven," she replied.

Her son thought a moment and then said, "And God threw him back down?"

It Wasn't My Fault!

• • • • • • • • • ANONYMOUS • • • • • • • • •

Insurance claim forms typically ask for a brief statement about how an accident happened. The combination of the small spaces on the forms and the finger-pointing instinct can lead to some curiously phrased explanations.

Car Accident Reports

- "A pedestrian hit me and went under my car."

- "The other car collided with mine without giving warning of its intention."

- "I had been learning to drive with power steering. I turned the wheel to what I thought was enough and found myself in a different direction going the opposite way."

- "Coming home, I drove into the wrong house and collided with a tree I don't have."

- "I thought my window was down, but found it was up when I put my hand through it."

- "No one was to blame for the accident, but it never would have happened if the other driver had been alert."

- "The pedestrian had no idea which direction to go, so I ran over him."

- "I saw the slow-moving, sad-faced old gentleman as he bounced off the hood of my car."
- "I had been driving for forty years when I fell asleep at the wheel and had an accident."
- "I was taking my canary to the hospital. It got loose in the car and flew out the window. The next thing I saw was his rear end, and there was a crash."
- "I was backing my car out of the driveway in the usual manner when it was struck by the other car in the same place where it had been struck several times before."
- "The indirect cause of this accident was a little guy in a small car with a big mouth."
- "The accident happened when the right door of a car came around the corner without giving a signal."
- "I was thrown from my car as it left the road. I was later found in a ditch by some stray cows."
- "I had been shopping for plants all day and was on my way home. As I reached an intersection, a hedge sprung up, obscuring my vision."
- "I was on the way to the doctor with rear end trouble when my universal joint gave way causing me to have an accident."
- "I was sure the old fellow would never make it to the other side of the road when I struck him."
- "I told the police that I was not injured, but on removing my hat, I found that I had a fractured skull."
- "I was unable to stop in time, and my car crashed into the other vehicle. The driver and passengers then left immediately for a vacation with injuries."

- "To avoid hitting the bumper of the car in front, I struck the pedestrian."
- "The accident occurred when I was attempting to bring my car out of a skid by steering it into the other vehicle."
- "When I could not avoid a collision, I stepped on the gas and crashed into the other car."
- "I collided with a stationary truck coming the other way."
- "In my attempt to kill a fly, I drove into a telephone pole."
- "My car was legally parked as it backed into the other vehicle."
- "As I approached the intersection, a stop sign suddenly appeared in a place where no stop sign had ever appeared before. I was unable to stop in time to avoid the accident."
- "The telephone pole was approaching fast. I was attempting to swerve out of its path when it struck my front end."
- "A truck backed though my windshield and into my wife's face."
- "I pulled away from the side of the road, glanced at my mother-in-law, and headed over the embankment."
- "The guy was all over the road. I had to swerve a number of times before I hit him."
- "An invisible car came out of nowhere, struck my vehicle, and vanished."

Choosing the Amusing

• • • • • • • • MARILYN MEBERG • • • • • • • •

When I was in the seventh grade, I had an experience in my sewing class which, if my person were evaluated on the basis of my performance, I would score a zero! I had come into the class optimistically expecting to master the art of sewing within the first few weeks. My confidence was reinforced by the teacher's promise that we could all become expert seamstresses by the end of the semester.

The first week of class was entitled "Knowing Our Machine." I soon discovered my machine had no desire to be known. In fact, it had no interest in a relationship whatsoever! I watched intently as our teacher demonstrated the intricate maze the thread had to follow from the spool to the needle. Every time I thought I had successfully completed each step and pressed the lever to begin the magical process of sewing, the thread would be slurped up by some unknown force and flail wildly about on the spool. Threading the machine was not the only difficulty I experienced.

To the left of the needle there is a little trap door where the bobbin lives. On the third day of class, for some inexplicable reason, my bobbin chose to fling itself out upon the floor and go racing across the room. The thread was bright red and left a tell-tale path to my machine. At this point my classmates gleefully assumed my ineptitude would provide them innumerable laughs

97

throughout the semester. The teacher, however, did not appear to relish that prospect. As she loomed over my machine with errant bobbin in hand, she said in carefully controlled tones, "Apparently we don't know our machine."

The second week of class was entitled "Knowing Our Pattern." Since my relationship with my machine was definitely not a friendly one, I approached my patterns with a bit of anxiety. In no time, patterns proved to be as great a mystery as machines. The paper was so thin and crinkly that the anxiety-induced perspiration on my hands caused the paper to stick to my palms so that I continually had to peel it off and use my elbow to position the pattern on the cloth. With this basic step finally accomplished, I was supposed to cut the cloth from around the pattern. I assumed that side A and side B were properly pinned and, when cut, would produce one piece; that's how it worked for everyone else. But somehow, when I unfolded the material, instead of a whole piece of fabric, I had side A in my left hand and side B in my right hand.

The project for the class was to make a pair of pajamas. I chose flannel fabric with little pink rosebuds. Perhaps you are aware that repeated ripping and sewing causes the threads in the fabric to separate and the design to become indistinguishable. It soon became impossible to discern if there were rosebuds, windmills, or frogs in the design.

As the semester progressed and I did not, I was in serious danger of failing. I was horrified—I had never failed a class before. I needed much more help than I felt free to ask for, because by now the teacher had adopted a certain stance toward me which was very disconcerting. She had the most peculiar response any time she saw me heading toward her desk with my fragile pajamas extended before me. She would begin to take in air, and the longer I remained at her desk the more she inhaled. There were times when I was sure she doubled in size, nearly filling her end of the room. Not only was I inhibited by this response, I was also unable to distinguish what she said as the sucked-in air whistled through her clenched teeth. I would usually flee from her desk in defeat and relief as the audible expulsion of breath signaled that she had once again survived her massive inhalations.

The day before the class was over everyone else had completed their project, but I was still working fervidly in an attempt to finish my pajamas. Shortly before the bell rang, I triumphantly put in the final stitch. I gingerly took the pajamas up to the teacher for her final inspection. To my dismay, through clenched teeth she ordered me to "Try them on." I did not think the fabric could withstand the pressure of my body. She was adamant, however, so I complied. I could not believe my eyes. I had sewn the left leg into the right arm and the right arm into the left leg. I tried every possible way to scrunch up my body so that maybe I could get by with them as they were, but one would have to have been far more deformed than I to pass them off as a good fit.

My friend, Jane, when she recovered from hysterics, promised to help me take out each wrong stitch with a straight pin after school and then pin the leg and the arm into their proper places. All I would have to do the next day was put in the final stitches. It seemed simple enough. The next day I settled down with my machine and began to sew very carefully. Within twenty minutes I had finished. I leaped jubilantly to my feet with the intention of rushing up to my teacher to show her my now completed project. In my haste, I neglected to pull the lever up to release the needle from the cloth. My sudden movement of jumping up without first releasing the pajamas knocked the machine off balance. As I stepped back from the falling machine, I realized I had inadvertently sewn my skirt into the pajama top so that I could not free myself from the material or the fall. I flew over the top of the machine as if I were on the end of a whip. I sprawled on the floor in final surrender to that piece of equipment, which had sought to defeat me all semester. My wonderful friends shrieked in hysterics; for once, the teacher did not begin her usual inhalations; she merely put her head down on her desk. Finally Jane cut me loose with giant pinking shears. I borrowed a skirt from the dressing room; Jane got my skirt out of my pajamas, sewed the leg and arm in properly, and the dismally frayed pajamas were turned in later that day. . . .

I soon began to laugh about my experience. My dad told me some weeks after the class was over that though he and Mom felt sorry for me as I muddled my way through sewing, they also had to exercise tremendous self-control as I would daily apprise them of my hard-to-believe errors. On several occasions they laughed uncontrollably when they were alone. Mom told me that she had never been able to grasp the details of sewing, absolutely abhorred the class she had to take in high school, and hoped never to see a sewing machine again. We began to laugh about the incidences from our respective classes until finally, one of our standing family jokes was to include a request for a sewing machine on our Christmas list each year. One of my Dad's favorite lines, even now, is to admire something I'm wearing and then with mock seriousness ask if I made it myself.

—from *Choosing the Amusing*

Hobbling Home

· · · · · · · · · SHEILA WALSH · · · · · · · · ·

*A bruised reed he will not break, and a smoldering
wick he will not snuff out. In faithfulness he will bring
forth justice; he will not falter or be discouraged till
he establishes justice on earth. (Isaiah 42:3–4 NIV)*

I used to think of myself as someone who didn't exercise regularly, but I realize now that can't be true, as I fly into the Dallas airport on a regular basis. Anyone who arrives in Dallas and has to catch a connecting flight faces an Olympian challenge.

One day I arrived at gate 2 in terminal A and my next flight left out of gate 43 in terminal C. My carry-on bags were heavier than usual, as I was doing research for a new book and had several study guides and commentaries in my briefcase. I looked to see how close I was to the underground rail transport and was delighted that I was only two gates away. As I approached the entrance, an official-looking woman with a very assertive smile stopped me.

"It's out of order today," she said, grinning from ear to ear.

"I'm not sure you should smile when you tell people that," I suggested. "It's misleading."

"Have a good day!" she insisted.

I walked over to the airport map muttering under my breath. It would have been impossible to walk any farther than I was going to have to walk that day. I had an hour before my flight, so I set off at a determined pace.

If we have met, you will know that I like to wear heels. I don't wear them because I think they make me look better or taller; I actually like them. When I wear flat shoes I feel like a duck, so most days I view the world from at least a three-inch advantage. That day I had on my purple suede boots. I dumped my bags on the floor of one of the moving walkways and stared out the window as black clouds began to fill the sky and large drops of rain pelted the tarmac. I prayed that my flight would not be canceled. I was tired and I just wanted to get home.

"Watch out!"

I turned to see who was yelling at me and promptly fell off the walkway.

"I was trying to warn you that it was coming to an end," an apologetic man said as he helped me up.

"Thanks!" I said with a weak smile. I tried to walk on and thought, *I don't remember having this limp this morning.*

I looked down and the heel of my right boot was gone, snapped clean off. I picked up the books that had scattered all over the place and tried to march forward with my left foot in a healthy boot and walk on my tiptoes with my defective right one. I looked totally ridiculous, like a drunken Long John Silver. After a few steps my calf hurt so badly that I reverted to hobbling, up and down, up and down. I caught sight of myself in the glass window of a store that I was limping past and started to laugh. I laughed so hard I had to put my bags down and hold on to the back of a chair.

My cell phone rang. It was my husband. I could hardly talk.

"Are you all right?" he asked.

"I'm great! I have two more miles to walk, it's starting to storm, and the heel broke off my boot," I spluttered.

"That does sound like fun," he said, not quite getting it.

There are days on our journey when all we can do is hobble, totter, and stagger along toward home . . . and that's okay. Because God will never falter, or even be discouraged, until He accomplishes all He has planned for us and His kingdom. We have a firm promise from God that even when it seems as if more than our heel is broken, He will watch over us. It may seem sometimes like we are close to a breaking point; but our hope is in a faithful God who says that although we may be bruised, we will not be broken. We may feel some days as if our light is dim and the storm gathering just outside our window threatens to extinguish it, but God promises that we will not be snuffed out.

So let's just keep our chins up and keep on hobbling.

—from *Irrepressible Hope*

For Laughs . . .

The Four Stages of Life:

1. You believe in Santa Claus.
2. You don't believe in Santa Claus.
3. You are Santa Claus.
4. You look like Santa Claus.

Which category do *you* belong in?

Part IV

Fit to Be Tied

· ·

Laughter Is the Spice of a Healthy Life

Laughter is inner jogging.

—NORMAN COUSINS

You better cut the pizza in four pieces because I'm not hungry enough to eat six.

—YOGI BERRA

The most remarkable thing about my mother is that for thirty years she served the family nothing but leftovers. The original meal has never been found.

—CALVIN TRILLIN

In Memoriam

• • • • • • • • • ANONYMOUS • • • • • • • • • •

It is with a heavy heart that I must pass on the following news. Please join me in remembering a great icon of the entertainment community:

The Pillsbury Doughboy died yesterday of a yeast infection and complications from repeated pokes in the belly. He was seventy-one years old. Doughboy was buried in a lightly greased coffin. Dozens of celebrities turned out to pay their respects, including Mrs. Butterworth, Hungry Jack, the California Raisins, the Hostess Twinkies, and Captain Crunch. The gravesite was piled high with flours. Aunt Jemima delivered the eulogy and lovingly described Doughboy as a man who never knew how much he was kneaded. Doughboy rose quickly in show business but his later life was filled with turnovers.

He was considered a very smart cookie, wasting much of his dough on half-baked schemes. Despite being a little flaky at times, he still, as a crusty old man, was considered a roll model for millions. Doughboy is survived by his wife, Play Dough, two children John Dough and Jane Dough, plus they had one in the oven. He is also survived by his elderly father, Pop Tart. The funeral was held at 3:50 for about twenty minutes.

Just So Much Fluff

• • • • • • • PATSY CLAIRMONT • • • • • • •

This is what the LORD says:
". . . Ask where the good way is,
and walk in it." (Jeremiah 6:16 NIV)

I awoke on New Year's Day and discovered I had been exceedingly generous to myself throughout the holidays. This was validated when I hefted my fluffy body onto the scales and watched the numbers tally. I usually avoid instruments that measure my body parts, partly because I don't want that much info and partly because I have a strong aversion to numbers. I am a math misfit. I much prefer words to numerical symbols—words are friendlier. And trust me, the sum total that glared up at me from the scale window was not the least bit hospitable. Add to that the problem with my jeans. Regardless of how I stretched or pulled on them, they did not want to meet in the middle and fasten.

"They must have shrunk," I told myself as I tugged on my britches.

"Cheap fabric," I mumbled while I grappled with the snap.

"Faulty design," I gasped as I sucked in my breath.

Just the effort of snapping the denim shut caused a swell of flesh to rise up and spill over my waistband. My midsection looked like a wave pool.

I could hardly continue to deny my dilemma with all that in-my-face information; I knew I needed a game plan. Unfortunately, my game plan didn't sound fun. Let me spell it for you: d-i-e-t. Been there? Done that? Me, too. Many times. So I should be an expert, but instead I tend to be a saboteur.

First I thought, *I shouldn't start my diet this week because I'm having a houseguest, and it wouldn't be friendly.* The following week I convinced myself I couldn't start then because I was going to fly west to our winter home in the desert, and travel is so disruptive to planned meals. Then I was busy settling into our condo, and I couldn't fit a food change into my busy days.

One morning I realized if I didn't just begin I would need to invest in an elastic company's stock. So I dragged my lagging attitude and my chubby carcass into my local diet center and started lifestyle changes. Besides consuming limited foods, I was encouraged to drink more water and to begin a walking program. Those two choices are not natural for me. But since I now had a financial investment in the program, as well as Cindy, a dear accountability person, to encourage me, I decided to give the changes an all-out effort. For ten days I obeyed the letter of the law. I ate only what was prescribed, I drank a lake, and I hoofed around my neighborhood.

Then came the weigh-in. I could hardly wait to be rewarded for my efforts. I slipped out of my shoes, hung my jacket over a nearby chair, and proudly stepped onto the scales.

Let me just say numbers are hostile and scales should be limited to fish. I had lost three ounces. Yes, you heard me right, *ounces.*

"Ounces?" I wailed at the weigh-in lady. "Ounces? Why, I could shave my legs and lose three ounces!"

Cindy tried to encourage me, "Maybe you lost inches."

"A three-ounce inch?" I wasn't comforted.

When I arrived home still whining, a thought slowly dawned on me: I had felt much better those past ten days. And the walking had knocked some of my mental cobwebs loose. Not to mention the boost to my self-esteem that came as I made healthier choices.

I decided to risk the jeans test. I found them and wiggled my way into them. Guess what? They snapped! Of course I couldn't breathe or bend, but any progress was appreciated. I figure three ounces of my waist slipped down into my shoes, giving me just enough clearance to snap the jeans closed. But my loafers were tight.

The following week, even though I was traveling, I stayed on the program. It was an effort, inconvenient, and may I say, worthwhile. Because at the next weigh-in I had dropped three—no, not ounces—for-real pounds. Now I can even boogie in my jeans. Well, okay, maybe I don't boogie, but I can snap and breathe a little.

I figure at this rate that in another month or two, maybe three, I'll once again be able to wear the clothes in the recesses of my closet. But what feels even better is that I'm making good choices that are benefiting my overall well-being in the here and now. I'm so grateful I finally woke up and headed in a fresh direction.

—from *The Great Adventure*

Release the Tension

• • • • • • • • JoAnna Harris • • • • • • • •

It's a lazy Sunday afternoon and I have big plans that involve watching a movie and eating ice cream. AJ—my health conscious, physically fit friend—suggests I accompany her to a yoga class. Yoga? Unless that's a cute nickname for frozen yogurt, I'm not interested. I'm sitting. I'm lounging. I'm lazy. She persists. She invites our friend Kat. Kat says, yoga? She's not interested. She's sitting. She's lounging. Kat and I make grand speeches to AJ about how we don't need yoga to feel rested. We don't want to work out on Sunday afternoon. We're tired. We're too busy. We have very very important things to attend to immediately. We said most of these things while climbing into AJ's SUV to join her at yoga.

I'm not what you would call a "work-out" girl. I don't own "work-out gear" or a snazzy sports bottle filled with liquid energy. I did buy a treadmill once, and ran on it about as many times. I exercise, I do. I just don't live and die by the early morning run. I'd rather shoot bamboo under my fingernails, actually. I don't join gyms. I don't own equipment. I don't attend Pilates classes or have a thigh master. But I'm on my way to yoga class with AJ and Kat. This should be a hoot.

We pull into the parking lot of the local YMCA, but it's not what you think. It's the swanky Y in the swanky part of the swanky side of town. The front doors open to more of a hotel lobby than a gym. I feel underdressed. Walking two steps in front of us is a fifty-year-old woman in an ankle length mink coat. I feel underdressed. Kat and I follow AJ through a maze of hallways and short stairwells. Meanwhile, we're all three trailing after Mink Coat exchanging puzzled smirks. Is she picking up a friend? Making a donation to the wing named after her late husband? Follow, follow, follow. Suddenly we all four round a corner and enter the yoga room. Kat, AJ, and I stop short as Mink Coat removes said article to reveal her head-to-toe red leotard. Uh-oh. Mink Coat is the teacher. I look around the room to see various people in various shapes and sizes bending and twisting and centering. Most of them are wearing trendy fashionable yoga gear. I look down and see that I'm wearing ratty old gym shorts and an eight-year-old sorority T-shirt. I feel underdressed.

AJ helps us locate yoga mats and we cower to the back of the room (not that it matters in a room made of mirrors). I try to "stretch" but end up pulling a muscle before class starts. Darn. An older gentleman enters the class wearing gray sweatpants pulled up to his armpits. I devilishly laugh—he doesn't know how to do yoga! Kat spies him as well. We are filled with cheer. Gray Sweatpants places his mat directly in front of me. Nice. I can out-yoga this joker before you can say Downward Dog pose.

It begins. We're told to breathe in and out—and that's about it. Kat and I feel somewhat relieved; shouldn't there be more? Mink Coat speaks in soothing tones that make me drowsy. Am I exercising? I mean, I've been to classes before but they all involved teachers who shouted into hands-free microphones while jumping around like their leotard was on fire. Exercise is supposed to be loud! Mink Coat purrs like a cat who's eaten an entire can of tuna. It's far too quiet in here. Will I sweat? I feel a bit chilly. Finally there are some instructions to raise our arms over our heads. Here we go. Mink Coat lulls us through a series of "poses" that make me feel rather silly. Kat and I keep grinning and making faces at AJ. Everyone else in the class is earnest and serious about the breathing and the bending; I'm just trying to stay upright. I'm watching Gray Sweatpants like a hawk. I will not be outdone by an old guy in an old T-shirt with old pit stains. As he bends, I bend further. Ha!

It's getting toward the end of class (I hope) and Mink Coat continues to sedate me with her orders. Release the tension seems to be an important one; she's been saying that one the most. Release the tension! Feel the earth energy! (What? . . . the earth what?) I'm standing with my feet hip-width apart and my head between my ankles. (Is my rear end showing?) The only feeling I'm feeling is the blood rushing to my brain. I'm trying to release the tension but I'm too tense about how to release it appropriately. I lift my head to see what Gray Sweatpants is doing just as Mink Coat hums at us to release the tension. Apparently Gray Sweatpants is good at following orders. He proceeds to release his tension right . . . in . . . my . . . face. The sound reverberates against the mirrored walls. It's so loud, I wonder if the people on the tennis courts think a thunderstorm is coming. I nearly collapse from the—is it polite to say odor? Smell? Horrific gaseous vapor? Gray Sweatpants doesn't seem fazed. Neither does anyone else for that matter. Maybe if I read *Yoga Phrases for Dummies* I would learn that "release the tension" means to let it *all* out. I look to my left and AJ is giggling. I look to my right and Kat is covering her mouth, holding in the heehaw. Me? I'm in a cloud of green smoke.

I haven't been back to yoga class.

Household Management for an Unmanageable Person

. . . . KATHY PEEL . . . .

The dinner hour at our house is another story from a different book. Oh, sure, the table is usually set in an enticing way with pretty dishes, colorful place mats, and cloth napkins. And our conversation is always lively as we recap the day and enjoy each other's company. But my cooking leaves a lot to be desired. Mainly a stomach pump. If there's ever a contest to find the world's worst cook, my family will make sure I'm a nominee. Even my neighbors harass me. When a fire truck roared down our street, they all ran to our house just sure I'd caught the kitchen on fire.

I thought my worries were over when Cajun cooking came into vogue. No cooking classes for me! No sirree. I already knew how to fix blackened chicken, blackened round steak, and blackened chocolate chip cookies. But the kids weren't fooled. They still prayed regularly for God to intervene in the situation. They were not sure, though, how He would answer their prayer. They figured either He would give them a supernatural ability to cook well, or I'd sell enough books so we could order in regularly. They're leaning toward the latter since my becoming a good cook falls into the category of Red Sea miracles.

Actually, my basic kitchen skills seem to be diminishing even as I write. Tonight at dinner, Bill and the boys complained that their hands were extremely dry and smelled like chlorine. "Kathy, what kind of soap are you using in the sink dispenser these days?" he inquired. Preoccupied with the mind-taxing job of trying to get dinner on the table, I answered, "I don't remember . . . the bottle's under the sink. Don't worry about it. Just carve the brisket."

As the boys cleaned up the kitchen, I heard a ruckus. Joel ran into the living room laughing hysterically. With more than a little sarcasm in his voice, he said, "Mom, you're such a whiz in the kitchen. You put automatic dishwasher detergent in the hand soap dispenser. No wonder we've lost three layers of skin!"

Yes, the boys were cleaning up the kitchen. And it's to someone's credit—I don't know whose—that they know the difference between dishwasher liquid and hand soap. But it's to my credit—and Bill's—that they do participate in our household management. They live here, after all. And I expect their future wives to thank me someday.

—from *Do Plastic Surgeons Take Visa?*
and Other Confessions of a Desperate Woman

Hungry?

• • • • • • • • • ANONYMOUS • • • • • • • • •

The following are actual signs seen by hungry eyes.

- *Open seven days a week. Closed Sundays.* On the bottom of a pizza parlor's take-out menu.

- *Parking for drive-through customers only.* A sign at a McDonald's in California.

- *We are handicapped-friendly. For example, if you are blind, we will read the menu for you.* A notice in a restaurant.

- *Eat Here—Get Gas.* A sign at a gas station.

- *Hot drinks to take out or sit in.* A sign in a café window.

- *You can't beat our meat!* A sign on a restaurant, now closed.

- *Please consume all food on premises.* A sign at a family-style restaurant.

- *Closed due to illness.* In a health food shop window.

- *After the tea break, staff should empty the teapot and stand upside down on the draining board.* In an office.

- *Toilet out of order. Please use floor below.* Spotted in the restroom of a restaurant building.

Celebrating Imagination

• • • • • • • • • LUCI SWINDOLL • • • • • • • • •

Once, when I was on yet another diet, I asked Marilyn to help me watch my weight, especially with sweets, for which I have a fatal weakness. During the first couple of weeks, everything went great. Lots of fish, chicken, cottage cheese, and lettuce. But on my way home from work one afternoon, I had an uncontrollable urge to drive by that Baskin-Robbins ice cream parlor near my house. "Life's too short," I thought, "to never have ice cream again." In no time I was lapping around the edge of a large scoop of "chocolate 'n peanut butter" on a lightly toasted sugar cone. Heavenly!

Late that evening, after Marilyn and I did a little shopping, I jokingly asked her if she'd like to stop by the ice cream parlor for a cone. Without the slightest hesitation, she responded, "Great idea! I was just thinking how delicious one would taste right now. Besides, you've been so good all this time, you deserve it. Come on, I'll buy."

As guilty as I felt, I just *couldn't* tell her. We drove along in silence, Marilyn no doubt relishing the idea of savoring ice cream, me praying fervently that the woman who waited on me earlier was no longer on duty. We got our ice cream (a different saleswoman was at the counter) and sat in the car, munching, licking, and making small talk. Then the brilliant idea hit me that it might be fun to confess my sin in some creative way. So I turned to Marilyn and said, "Hey, Mar, if you can tell me what I'm thinking about this Baskin-Robbins store, I'll take you to see that musical we've been wanting to go to."

"What? Is that it? No hints?"

"No hints. You get three guesses. Come on, Mar, you can do it. Just what I'm thinking."

"Fat chance." I winced when she said that. "Okay, Luci, my first guess is that you've decided to have your picture made right here in front of the store for your new book. Everybody will see how festive you are and will want to buy the book."

"Great guess! That's fabulous! It's wrong, but it's such a good guess!"

After a few more minutes of intense concentration, Marilyn said, "All right. My second guess is that you have made arrangements to work in this ice cream parlor for one week in order to gather stories for your book. Right?"

I grinned again. "Wrong again, pal. But your guesses are so vivid. Shows you're really using the ol' imagination."

Suddenly, she blurted out, "This is outrageous, I know, but since I only have one more guess, I'll shoot in the dark. Here's number three: You've already been in here once today for ice cream. Chocolate. You didn't want to tell me earlier because you were embarrassed since you had asked me to help you stick to your diet. And then when I answered 'yes' when you asked if I wanted to come here, you were so caught off guard that you decided to go along with it anyway like nothing had happened. That's why you ordered lemon ice cream. You already had chocolate once today. Besides, lemon is nearer your diet and you thought I'd be proud of you if I heard you order lemon instead of chocolate."

I stared at her with my half-eaten cone poised in midair. "Well???"

"Marilyn, this is *unreal!* I can't believe it! How did you guess that? *I'm* the only one who could know all those details. Boy is this spooky. A regular Steven Spielberg production."

She was roaring with laughter. It seems that the woman who had waited on me earlier in the day was the mother of a school friend of Marilyn's daughter, Beth. In a casual conversation at the grocery store, the woman innocently mentioned to Marilyn that I had been in that afternoon for an ice cream cone. She had recognized me from church and knew that Marilyn and I were friends. Marilyn decided not to mention the incident to me, but thought she'd beat me at my own game. What an imagination that woman has! She played along from start to finish! I loved it!

Let your imagination run wild and think up new ways to add spice to your life.

—from *You Bring the Confetti, God Brings the Joy*

The Things Kids Say

• • • • • • • • • ANONYMOUS • • • • • • • • • •

The Bible school teacher asked, "Now, Billy, tell me, do you say prayers before eating?" "No sir," he replied. "We don't have to. My mom is a great cook!"

Children were lined up in the cafeteria of a Catholic school for lunch. At the head of the table was a large pile of apples.

The nun made a note: "Take only one, God is watching."

At the other end of the table, was a large pile of chocolate chip cookies. A boy wrote a note saying, "Take all you want, God is watching the apples."

My wife invited some people over for dinner. After everyone was seated at the table, she turned to our six-year-old daughter and said, "Would you like to say the blessing?"

"I wouldn't know what to say," our daughter replied.

"Just say what you hear Mommy say, okay?" my wife said.

Our daughter bowed her head and said, "Dear Lord, why on earth did I invite all these people over for dinner?"

Exercise Advice

• • • • • • • • • MARK LOWRY • • • • • • • • •

Who invented exercise? Why do our bodies need it? Mine has done just fine without it for over thirty years. I know our bodies are the temples of the Lord, but show me where Jesus ever jogged. We have no record of the Lord doing sit-ups. None whatsoever. Everywhere in the Bible that it talks about the Lord's mode of transportation, it says He either walked or rode a donkey.

Jesus didn't *run* on the water. He walked on the water.

Paul said that physical exercise profiteth little. I agree with him. Every time I've ever exercised, it profited very little.

All right, I'll admit it. I did try jogging once. I went all out too. I bought some very expensive sweats. I spent ten to fifteen dollars on the tennis shoes alone. I even bought a sweatband for my head. What I needed was a sweatband for my body. I hate to sweat.

That fateful morning, I put on my sweats, tromped outside, and tried to jog around the block. I did okay for the first forty-five seconds. Then my heart started racing. My heart hadn't felt like that since I ran the thirty-six-minute mile in high school.

(That was probably the *Guinness Book of Records* entry for the event. By the time I came in from that race, all the other kids had showered, shaved, and were halfway home.)

Still, I was out there—jogging. Blisters were forming inside those ten-dollar sneakers, and I figured my heart was supposed to feel like it was pumping blood for the whole county. By the time

I'd gotten to the third house down from mine, my sweatpants, sweatshirt, and sweatband were totally soaked with sweat. All I needed was a bar of soap, and I could've skipped the shower. Then my side started feeling like someone had snuck up behind me and stuck a hot poker into it.

I doubled over somewhere near house number four.

Through my legs, I saw some little kids waiting on the school bus. There was one little snotty-nosed kid smacking his lips. He was pointing at me, saying, "Hey, maybe that guy'll drop dead, and we can try out the CPR we learned yesterday at school!"

I gave him the dirtiest look I could muster, the same one I'd been giving everything since I left my house.

When I finally got back home, I put my tennis shoes away. I haven't seen them since. I threw my sweatpants in the corner of my closet. They're still standing there. My sweatband has crystallized and is making a nice salt block for the neighbor's cat.

I haven't totally given up on exercise.

My dad's always said he was gonna start jogging just as soon as he passes a jogger with a smile on his face.

I've seen those beautiful bodies on the talk shows. And I must admit those people look really good. But when they're asked how many hours a day they spend in the gym, the answer is always two to three hours every single day!

Who has two to three hours a day to spend in the gym? I certainly don't.

Instead, I just tuck that extra fat roll deeper into my pants. It may be getting harder and harder to hold in my stomach, but it doesn't take two to three hours a day.

Yet.

—from *Out of Control*

Roughing It

• • • • • • • • • ANONYMOUS • • • • • • • • •

America's Forest Service allows hikers and campers the opportunity to give feedback by writing down any comments, in the hopes of improving future trips. These are some of the less helpful suggestions.

- "Escalators would help on steep uphill sections."
- "A small deer came into my camp and stole my bag of pickles. Is there a way I can get reimbursed? Please call."
- "Trails need to be wider so people can walk while holding hands."
- "Too many bugs and leeches and spiders and spiderwebs. Please spray the wilderness to rid the area of these pests."
- "Ban walking sticks in wilderness. Hikers that use walking sticks are more likely to chase animals."
- "Found a smoldering cigarette left by a horse."
- "Trails need to be reconstructed. Please avoid building trails that go uphill."
- "Chairlifts need to be in some places so that we can get to wonderful views without having to hike to them."
- "The coyotes made too much noise last night and kept me awake. Please eradicate these annoying animals."

- "Please pave the trails so they can be plowed of snow in the winter."

- "Reflectors need to be placed on trees every fifty feet so people can hike at night with flashlights."

- "A McDonald's would be nice at the trailhead."

- "All the mile markers are missing this year."

- "Instead of a permit system or regulations, the Forest Service needs to reduce worldwide population growth to limit the number of visitors to wilderness."

- "The places where trails do not exist are not well marked."

- "Too many rocks in the mountains."

- "Need more signs to keep area pristine."

The Truth About Dentists

• • • • • • • • LEWIS GRIZZARD • • • • • • •

Nearly every society has had its element of cruel and sadistic monsters, preying on the helpless and innocent. We call ours "dentists."

Get ready for this, because I don't want you to be caught off guard. The American Dental Association has launched a new propaganda scheme aimed at people who will do anything to stay out of a dentist's office—people like me.

We are no small group. According to its own figures, the ADA says only half the population goes to the dentist each year.

The purpose of its scheme is to get the other 50 percent strapped into that chair so the dentist can scrape and pull and drill and make the poor suckers hurt and bleed and then charge them for his trouble.

The scheme includes sending out ADA "ambassadors" all over the country to tell you incredible lies, such as, it doesn't hurt to go to the dentist anymore.

One of those "ambassadors" is a lady dentist named Dr. Sheva Rapoport, of Allentown, Pennsylvania. I read a newspaper account of some of the baloney she is peddling.

Get a load of this song and dance. According to Dr. Rapoport:

- Dentists' offices now offer a more pleasant environment than before.

- Dentists are now more aware of their patients' feelings.

- Dental equipment has been improved.

- If you ask for one, a dentist will provide a cost estimate before he starts excavating in your mouth.

Big deal. So dentists have put in Muzak and hung a few pictures, and now you can find out about their outrageous prices ahead of time.

What the ADA wants to do is to double root-canal sales, and I, for one, will not be fooled by its would-be clever trick.

Do not listen to the ADA, America. Listen to your Uncle Lewis, who knows all there is to know about dentists, because he was held prisoner by one until he was old enough to escape without parental consent.

The *truth* about dentists—clip and save:

- Of course, it still hurts to go to the dentist, because dentists *want* it to hurt. They like to watch you squirm, they like to hear your muffled cries of agony, they like to fill your mouth with cotton and then ask you, So who do you like Monday night? The Cowboys or the Steelers?

- Dental equipment will be improved only when the heinous drill is totally silent, has a rubber tip, and tickles, rather than feels like someone has taken to your mouth with the first cousin to a jackhammer.

- When a dentist says, "This may sting a little," he really means, "How high can you jump?"

- Oral Roberts University is not a school of dentistry.

- Beware any dentist whose nickname is "Mad Dog" or "Nick the Grinder."
- Beware any dentist with a nervous twitch.
- Beware any dentist who is missing one or more fingers.
- Beware any dentist who is wearing an inordinate amount of leather and whose chair has straps.
- Beware dating dental assistants. They kiss with their teeth, and floss in public.
- Despite what the American Dental Association says, there are worse things than having all your teeth rot out.
- I would gladly list a couple, but it's late and I have to go gum dinner.

—from *Won't You Come Home, Billy Bob Bailey?*

How Can I Be Over the Hill When
I Never Even Got to the Top?

• • • • • • • • BARBARA JOHNSON • • • • • • • •

Wherever I go, women agree that two of their least favorite subjects are *aging* and *dieting*. My advice is to not let either one steal your joy. I decided a long time ago to stop fretting over increasing years and extra pounds and relish each day instead.

That doesn't mean I ignore healthy eating, nor does it mean that I seldom exercise. Before having diabetes made exercise a must for me, I was not a real enthusiast about working out. My idea of exercise was a good, brisk sit, or maybe wrestling with the cellophane wrapper on a Twinkie.

To paraphrase the bumper "snicker," every time I thought about exercise, I would lie down until the thought went away. Or Bill and I would ride our bikes—right down to the corner dough-nut shop in the morning for coffee and maple bars. . . .

Keeping weight down is a constant struggle for so many of us. Fighting the battle of the bulges is like holding a beach ball under water all your life. If you relax for just one minute, POW! Up it goes. Then it's a big struggle to get that ball back under the water again.

It seems that most of the time you're being forced to eat like a rabbit. After all, when you take all the fat, sugar, salt, and starch out of life, what's left except stuff that's high in tasteless fiber?

My friend, Lynda, read about a fabulous idea for weight control. Doctors give you a balloon to swallow and then it is inflated in your stomach. Because the balloon keeps your stomach feeling "full," you don't want to eat and, of course, you lose weight. However, there is one *string* attached—literally! It is tied to the balloon and then extends back up the esophagus and hangs out the nose! (It seems the string is important in case the balloon breaks or there is some other emergency.)

Lynda and I began brainstorming on what we would do if we swallowed one of these balloons and had the string hanging out of our noses. What if one of our grandchildren decided to pull on it? Or what if it got caught in our toothbrushes?

Then we got a brilliant idea. Why not tie a brightly colored bead on the end of the string and let it dangle there, making a fashion statement? When you became tired of that, you could try stuffing the string up your nose out of sight, but then it would undoubtedly itch and eventually you'd sneeze and out the string would pop! If you were having trouble getting conversation started at some get-together that bead would surely do the trick!

The balloon idea sounded glorious except for that stupid string. Too bad. Lynda and I finally decided it was another miracle cure down the tube, or maybe you'd have to say up the nose. Whatever, we decided to skip on swallowing a balloon and keep on wrestling with the beach ball as best we can.

—from *Splashes of Joy in the Cesspools of Life*

Chasing Pots

• • • • • • • • • THELMA WELLS • • • • • • • • •

When I think about a fork I seldom think about a fork in the road. I think about a fork in my mouth. I know what "fork in the road" means: it's an opportunity to change. So, let me tell you about an opportunity to change that came my way early in life.

You've heard about the proverbial pot of gold at the end of the rainbow. When I was a young girl, that was a common expression. It was meant to encourage us to work hard, doing all we could to get rich, successful, happy, or whatever we thought were the goodies in the pot waiting for us at the end of our efforts.

Now, looking for the "pot of gold" can sometimes be a noble enterprise. But from my earliest memory, I found myself chasing quite different pots: pans, skillets, cookie sheets, and grills, to be exact. I would place the goodies from those pots on plates, saucers, cups, and bowls, and my best friends were the forks or spoons that were jet-propelled from those goody holders to my mouth. Chasing food became a great adventure.

My pot-chasing days started when I was a little girl at my great-grandmother's table where breakfast was a must. Bacon, eggs, grits, toast, pancakes, waffles, homemade jelly, butter, juice, and milk were an everyday beginning. Lunch was a meat sandwich with everything but the kitchen sink or some kind of homemade soup or stew. And dinner was always three courses, often with several dishes like chicken-fried steak, ham, roast, lamb chops, turkey, oxtails, neck bones, fried chicken, mashed potatoes, corn, collard greens, turnip greens, mustard greens, string beans, new potatoes, sweet potatoes, squash, macaroni and cheese, black-eyed peas, homemade rolls, corn bread, butter, jelly, and a scrumptious dessert.

No wonder I chased the contents of the containers on the stove. The stuff that was served up from them was too good to let spoil. I took my eating instructions seriously. "Eat all your food. I ain't got food to throw away!" So rather than be scolded for not eating with gusto, I gladly obliged.

Chasing pots and pans brought predictable results. Pouring in all those goodies made me a statistic of obesity at the age of nine. I was so fat that the doctors at Freeman's clinic in Dallas had to put me in the hospital and reduce me to my normal weight. A layer of fat had covered my heart, and I had become a candidate for living above the rainbow in the Third Heaven, never to chase another pot again.

Within ten days, under medical supervision, I started to feel like a little girl who could more easily run, jump, and enjoy breathing when I played. After that fork in the road, my great-grandmother altered her feeding style dramatically. I kept my weight normal until I had my first child.

When people told me I needed to eat for two, I took them literally. After my baby was born, I had all but doubled my weight. . . . I was headed straight to the end of the road of health, and I didn't know how to take the better fork.

Today, at over sixty years of age, I've finally found a recipe in the weight-loss/get-healthy pot that's made a difference in my life. The fork is now pointed in the right direction for me. I received great advice from my daughter Vikki after she and others had tried Dr. Peter J. D'Adamo's "eating right for your blood type" approach with stunning success. Actually, it's the most sensible and easiest eating arrangement I have ever tried. I'm eating almost all the fruits, veggies, fish, whole-grain breads, and other delicious foods I want. Eating has become an adventure again, but this time the results are positive: I'm more mentally alert, have more energy, and experience less stress. I've reduced my cooking time, my skin is clearing, my eyesight has improved, my hypertension is stabilized, and I've lost weight without really thinking about it.

Take it from me: Chasing the fat found in the pots on the stove will leave you feeling frumpy, fit to be tied, and fighting back tears. But there is another pot that contains all the fixings of the true fulfillment we seek. Although the contents of this pot can cause growth and increase, these goodies never make us obese. Quite the contrary: The more we eat, the more we need to eat. The ingredients feed our spirit, mind, and soul. When consumed correctly, the goodies in this pot never cause depression, stress, anxiety, agitation, aggravation, anger, or anything distasteful or destructive. We can eat this food any time of day or night without regretful results. We never have to put a lid on this pot or place where it won't spoil. It remains fresh day after day, year after year. Everybody's blood type is completely compatible with the contents of this pot. No more dieting. No more deprivation. No more disillusionment. All we have to do is dip into the pot, ladle out what we want to chew on, swallow it, let it grow on us, then share it with someone else. The brand name of this pot is the Holy Bible. I call it the Pot of Testaments.

When you come to a fork in the road, take it, taste it, try it. You'll like it!

—from *The Great Adventure*

Life Is a Beautiful Thing

• • • • • • • • • Luci Swindoll • • • • • • • • •

To grow older joyfully also means to accept what is. This implies we determine to live with the reality that says we are truly the age we are, to date. Any age is beautiful because life itself is a beautiful thing. As Mark Twain once said, "Age is mostly a matter of mind. If you don't mind, it doesn't matter." Where we get into trouble is the attempt to be something we are not, whether that's in our age or in our person. Such inner deception can also lead to self-defeat and depression.

We are the most appealing to others, and the happiest within, when we are completely ourselves. But it is a constant struggle because, as Scripture teaches, the world is always trying to press us into its mold. The mold of the world is the mold of the synthetic, the mold of the artificial, the mold of the celluloid—the "Plastic Person." The world cries, "You've got to be thin and you've got to be rich. You've got to be great." But Scripture says, "You don't have to be any of those things. You simply have to be yourself—at any age as God made you, available to Him so that He can work in and through you to bring about His kingdom and His glory." Now relax. Trust Him and be yourself. It certainly isn't easy, but it is possible.

—from *You Bring the Confetti, God Brings the Joy*

For Laughs . . .

Who says riding an elevator has to be boring? There are all kinds of ways to make an everyday elevator ride the most interesting part of your day.

Things to Do in an Elevator

❀ Crack open your briefcase or purse, and while peering inside ask, "Got enough air in there?"

❀ Offer nametags to everyone getting on the elevator. Wear yours upside down.

❀ Stand silent and motionless in the corner, facing the wall, without getting off when the doors open.

❀ When arriving at your floor, grunt and strain to yank the doors open, then act embarrassed when they open by themselves.

❀ Greet everyone getting on the elevator with a warm handshake. Look them in the eye and say, "Welcome aboard! Just call me admiral."

❀ Bet the other passengers you can fit a quarter up your nose.

❀ Say "Ding!" as you pass each floor.

❀ Draw a little square on the floor with chalk and announce to the other passengers that this is your personal space.

❀ Make race car noises when anyone gets on or off.

❀ Whistle "It's a Small World" incessantly.

❀ Sell Girl Scout cookies.

❀ On the highest floor, hold the door open and demand that it stay open until you hear the penny you dropped down the shaft go *plink* at the bottom.

❀ Meow occasionally.

❀ Start a sing-along.

❀ Listen to the elevator walls with a stethoscope.

❀ Pull your gum out of your mouth in long strings.

Part V

Till Death
(or Insanity) Do Us Part

●●

Laughter Is the Spice of Life in Love

Love: a temporary insanity curable by marriage.

—AMBROSE BIERCE

Keep your eyes wide open before marriage, half shut afterwards.

—BENJAMIN FRANKLIN

An archaeologist is the best husband a woman can have; the older she gets, the more interested he is in her.

—AGATHA CHRISTIE

Why Can't You Be Like Me?

• • • • • • • • JOEY O'CONNOR • • • • • • • •

Men and women are different. Unique. They think, perceive, act, talk, and respond to situations in different ways. This was a major revelation to me. A startling breakthrough. . . .

In my research, I also learned that men and women are different in every cell of their bodies. Evidently, some chromosomes began dating in order to find suitable mates. The guy chromosome always said he'd call, but never did. One particular female chromosome decided men are jerks and that she'd had enough. She put her foot down (X), and men have never had another leg to stand on since (Y).

It's a good thing that the differences between men and women exist at the most basic elements of human life. Can you imagine for a moment what would happen if a single male cell ever resided in a female body? . . . Women would finally see what it's like to take the trash out in rain, sleet, and snow. They'd have to admit fault for any argument and apologize for just about everything except breathing. Upon arriving home from a long day at the office, they would take one look at the house and ask stupid questions like, "What have you been doing all day long?" Insensitive and rash, women would communicate in grunts, shrugs, sign language, and mental telepathy. They'd be completely clueless on how to change a diaper. Pretending to be eighteen years old again, women would transform into weekend warriors twisting ankles, pulling hamstrings, complaining about their backs, and only visiting the doctor if involved in a major auto accident. Worst of all, women would control the remote! Aaaahhhhh!

If you want a really scary thought regarding this Frankenstein-like genetic reengineering, what if a single female cell were planted inside the bodies of men? Every two-car garage in every neighborhood throughout America would become a giant closet! Ice-skating, softball, and synchronized swimming would be the only sports on television. Men would change eight times before finally wearing the first outfit they tried on. They'd watch "chick flicks." When Mom is away, the kids would be clean, well-groomed, and fed from the four basic food groups instead of eating Happy Meals and Froot Loops all weekend long. Guys would go to the bathroom in twos, threes, or small groups of one hundred.

Burping and passing gas in public would be history. Men would start asking no-win questions like, "Do you like my outfit?" "How do you like my haircut?" and "Do I look fat?" Males would no longer be macho, strong, competitive, analytical, opinionated types, but instead they'd be sensitive, caring, nurturing, and intuitively smart. With that single female cell, men would cry watching soaps and get angry at those other dumb men on *Oprah.* They'd also discover the joys of PMS—*what vengeance!* Unable to handle the rigors of childbirth, all men would go straight for an epidural as they smoke cigars and play poker while waiting for a C-section. Most important, the toilet seat would always be put back down.

Thank God there's no X in Y chromosomes and no Y in X chromosomes. What a scary mix!

—from *Women Are Always Right and Men Are Never Wrong*

I Do

● ● ● ● ● ● GEORGE BERNARD SHAW ● ● ● ● ● ●

When two people are under the influence of the most violent, most insane, most delusive, and most transient of passions, they are required to swear that they will remain in that excited, abnormal, and exhausting condition continuously until death do them part.

—from *Getting Married*

Sound Advice

Kids from the ages of five to ten were asked questions about what they thought of dating. Here are some of the more enlightening responses.

The Purpose of Dating:

- "On the first date, they just tell each other lies, and that usually gets them interested enough to go for a second date." *(Mike, age ten)*
- "One of the people has freckles, and so he finds somebody else who has freckles too." *(Andrew, age six)*
- "Dates are for having fun, and people should use them to get to know each other. Even boys have something to say if you listen long enough." *(Lynnette, age eight)*

What To Do When a First Date Turns Sour:

- "I'd run home and play dead. The next day I would call all the newspapers and make sure they wrote about me in all the dead columns." *(Craig, age nine)*

How to Make Someone Fall in Love with You:

- "Tell them that you own a whole bunch of candy stores." *(Del, age six)*

- "Yell out that you love them at the top of your lungs . . . and don't worry if their parents are right there." *(Manuel, age eight)*

- "Don't do things like have smelly, green sneakers. You might get attention, but attention ain't the same thing as love." *(Alonzo, age nine)*

- "One way is to take the girl out to eat. Make sure it's something she likes to eat. French fries usually work for me." *(Bart, age nine)*

- "It isn't always how you look. Look at me. I'm handsome like anything, and I haven't got anybody to marry me yet." *(Brian, age seven)*

What Most People Are Thinking When They Say "I Love You":

- "The person is thinking: 'Yeah, I really do love him. But I hope he showers at least once a day.'" *(Michelle, age nine)*

- "Some daters might be real nervous, so they are glad that they finally got it out and said it, and now they can go eat." *(Dick, age seven)*

Worth of a Rib

• • • • • • • • • ANONYMOUS • • • • • • • • •

Adam was walking around the Garden of Eden feeling very lonely, so God asked Adam, "What is wrong with you?"

Adam said, "I don't have anyone to talk to."

God said, "I was going to give you a companion, and it would be a woman."

God continued: "This person will cook for you and wash your clothes. She will always agree with every decision you make. She will bear your children and never ask you to get up in the middle of the night to take care of them. She won't nag you, and will always be the first to admit she was wrong when you've had a disagreement. She will never have a headache, and will freely give you love and compassion whenever needed."

Adam asked God, "What would a woman like this cost me?"

God said, "An arm and a leg."

Adam then asked, "What can I get for just a rib?"

You Did This for Me?

He deserves our compassion. When you see him, do not laugh. Do not mock. Do not turn away or shake your head. Just gently lead him to the nearest bench and help him sit down.

Have pity on the man. He is so fearful, so wide-eyed. He's a deer on the streets of Manhattan. Tarzan walking through the urban jungle. He's a beached whale, wondering how he got here and how he'll get out.

Who is this forlorn creature? This ashen-faced orphan? He is—please remove your hats out of respect—he is the man in the women's department. Looking for a gift.

The season may be Christmas. The occasion may be her birthday or their anniversary. Whatever the motive, he has come out of hiding. Leaving behind his familiar habitat of sporting goods stores, food courts, and the big-screen television in the appliance department, he ventures into the unknown world of women's wear. You'll spot him easily. He's the motionless one in the aisle. Were it not for the sweat rings under his arms, you'd think he was a mannequin.

But he isn't. He is a man in a woman's world, and he's never seen so much underwear. At the Wal-Mart where he buys his, it's all wrapped up and fits on one shelf. But here he is in a forest of lace. His father warned him about places like this. Though the sign above says "linger-ie," he knows he shouldn't.

147

So he moves on, but he doesn't know where to go. You see, not every man has been prepared for this moment as I was. My father saw the challenge of shopping for women as a rite of passage, right in there with birds and bees and tying neckties. He taught my brother and me how to survive when we shopped. I can remember the day he sat us down and taught us two words. To get around in a foreign country, you need to know the language, and my father taught us the language of the ladies' department.

"There will come a time," he said solemnly, "when a salesperson will offer to help you. At that moment take a deep breath and say this phrase, '*Es-tée Lau-der.*'" On every gift-giving occasion for years after, my mom received three gifts from the three men in her life: Estée Lauder, Estée Lauder, and Estée Lauder.

My fear of the women's department was gone. But then I met Denalyn. Denalyn doesn't like Estée Lauder. Though I told her it made her smell motherly, she didn't change her mind. I've been in a bind ever since.

This year for her birthday I opted to buy her a new dress. When the salesperson asked me Denalyn's size, I said I didn't know. I honestly don't. I know I can wrap my arm around her and that her hand fits nicely in mine. But her dress size? I never inquired. There are certain questions a man doesn't ask.

The woman tried to be helpful. "How does she compare to me?" Now, I was taught to be polite to women, but I couldn't be polite and answer the question. There was only one answer, "She is thinner."

I stared at my feet, looking for a reply. After all, I write books. Surely I could think of the right words.

I considered being direct: "She is less of you."

Or complimentary: "You are more of a woman than she is."

Perhaps a hint would suffice? "I hear the store is *downsizing.*"

Finally I swallowed and said the only thing I knew to say, "Estée Lauder?"

She pointed me in the direction of the perfume department, but I knew better than to enter. I would try the purses. Thought it would be easy. What could be complicated about selecting a tool for holding cards and money? I've used the same money clip for eight years. What would be difficult about buying a purse?

Oh, naive soul that I am. Tell an attendant in the men's department that you want a wallet, and you're taken to a small counter next to the cash register. Your only decision is black or brown. Tell an attendant in the ladies' department that you want a purse, and you are escorted to a room. A room of shelves. Shelves with purses. Purses with price tags. Small but potent price tags . . . prices so potent they should remove the need for a purse, right?

I was pondering this thought when the salesperson asked me some questions. Questions for which I had no answer. "What kind of purse would your wife like?" My blank look told her I was clueless, so she began listing the options: "Handbag? Shoulder bag? Glove bag? Backpack? Shoulder pack? Change purse?"

Dizzied by the options, I had to sit down and put my head between my knees lest I faint. Didn't stop her. Leaning over me, she continued, "Moneybag? Tote bag? Pocketbook? Satchel?"

"Satchel?" I perked up at the sound of a familiar word. Satchel Paige pitched in the major leagues. This must be the answer. I straightened my shoulders and said proudly, "Satchel."

Apparently she didn't like my answer. She began to curse at me in a foreign language. Forgive me for relating her vulgarity, but she was very crude. I didn't understand all she said, but I do know she called me a "Dooney Bird" and threatened to "brighten" me with a spade that belonged to someone named Kate. When she laid claim to "our mawny," I put my hand over the wallet in my hip pocket and defied, "No, it's my money." That was enough. I got out of there as fast as I could. But as I left the room, I gave her a bit of her own medicine. "Estée Lauder!" I shouted and ran as fast as I could.

Oh, the things we do to give gifts to those we love.

But we don't mind, do we? We would do it all again. Fact is, we *do* it all again. Every Christmas, every birthday, every so often we find ourselves in foreign territory. Grownups are in toy stores. Dads are in teen stores. Wives are in the hunting department, and husbands are in the purse department.

Not only do we enter unusual places, we do unusual things. We assemble bicycles at midnight. We hide the new tires with mag wheels under the stairs. One fellow I heard about rented a movie theater so he and his wife could see their wedding pictures on their anniversary.

And we'd do it all again. Having pressed the grapes of service, we drink life's sweetest wine—the wine of giving. We are at our best when we are giving. In fact, we are most like God when we are giving.

—from *He Chose the Nails*

When "The One" Turns Out to Be Just Someone

• • • • • • • • JoAnna Harris • • • • • • • • •

I'll start out by telling a little about myself. I love to watch TV and drink way too much Diet Coke. I have a lifelong love affair with French fries. I love to read really good books and sometimes I even like to read bad ones. I tend to be cliquish accidentally, which causes people to think I'm snobby. I'm a world champion Nertz player—at least among my friends. I'm more spicy than sweet, with food and with life. Lately, I've become an avid treadmill runner and I'm turning thirty this year. Oh yeah, and my fiancé broke up with me two months before our wedding date. That about sums it up.

Isn't it funny that the sentences that affect us most are typically the shortest? You got the job. You're fired. I met someone else. I'm pregnant. There's been an accident. We won. We lost. Wanna go out? Will you marry me? We need to talk. I love you. I hate you. And the best one of all . . . I have to tell you something. Nothing good ever comes from someone saying they have to tell you something. Good news tends to burst right out. Bad news usually needs a setup. Something like—I have to tell you something. A short sentence that recently changed my life's direction was—I think it's too soon. Meaning too soon for us to proceed with the wedding in two months. This coming from the man who had asked me to

151

marry him months earlier. I had a ring and everything. Forget the ring, I had it all. The dress, the church, the bridesmaids, the flowers, the invitations, the food, the musicians. . . . I guess he changed his mind. I guess he got scared. I still don't really know.

I remember everything about him and me and the room and the temperature and his face. But I still don't know how it happened. He just said it. And I knew it would change my life. We were sitting on the couch in his apartment. I felt like the couch was made of crackling bubble wrap and if I made any sudden movements he would scurry away. I wanted to lunge at him. Beg him not to do this. Command him to snap out of it. Find out where he was and demand that this impostor in front of me bring back the real guy I fell in love with. I wanted to be an action movie star and jump on my motorcycle and ride to freedom, never looking back. I wanted to fly backwards around the world like Superman and turn back time. I wanted to say all the right things. But all I could manage was good-bye.

I have a white dress. I have the perfect white dress and the perfect veil. It's my Aunt Beverlee's veil that my grandmother handmade twenty-seven years ago. It's exquisite and breathtaking. I was going to be wearing that perfect white dress and walk down the aisle to the perfect song on the perfect day surrounded by perfect flowers and perfect candles—and marry the perfect guy. I had never been so sure of anything in my life. I was so sure, in fact, that I quit my fulfilling job, said good-bye to my irreplaceable friends and family, and moved from Tennessee to Maine. I moved to Maine to be near the man of my dreams . . . the one I could see smiles and laughter and babies and grandbabies and comfort and safety with. My fairy tale was coming true. The day I had thought about my entire life. It was really happening. Everything I had ever wished for—he was. Everything I had longed to hear—he said. I had finally found The One. My match. I lived in Maine a total of seven days. Seven days. How can a love that would last a lifetime unravel in seven days?

The white dress is still hanging in the closet. The flowers and candles were canceled. The musicians were told not to come. And I'm expected to survive and keep living and go on without. I guess I should be glad I'm not on a TV reality dating show and all of America isn't concerned about how the relationship is going. Although, sometimes it does feel as if there are millions of onlookers. It's left me with more than a broken heart. It's left me wondering what it truly means to love someone. I watch TV couples profess undying *love*—not attraction or like or you're-kinda-cool. They promise to love each other forever. Do they really know what love means? Do they really understand? Do I? I thought I did. I thought I had found what my heart had always longed for. Thought I had found forever. But in reality— the real reality without cameras and producers and editing—I didn't. That is the reality that I must face every day.

I get nervous that maybe I made it up. That he only loved me in my head. That I had done it again. That I had convinced myself he was my soul mate when really he was just some guy. It's like the dangling carrot, this elusive "soul mate." At least to me. People talk about it as if it's a course you should take in college or a learn-at-home tutorial. A rite of passage. Finding The One. Sounds like an Indiana Jones movie. I'd like to know the rules, since I seem to be so bad at it.

Can there be more than one? Is it possible to meet one soul mate and then another one? Is a soul mate only the person you marry? And if that's true—what is a soul mate? I wouldn't know, never having found one. I thought I did. Twice. What's so wrong with me that I could get such a huge thing wrong—twice. Ugh. Just the thought of it makes me queasy. Girls in the movies can meet and "just know" someone is their soul mate in a span of 110 minutes on screen. I can't seem to do it in my lifetime.

It's interesting to me how relationships start. Especially the big ones. The ones that change your life and your perspective. The ones people write songs about. (And books.) My parents met at church. My mom had been a churchgoer her whole life and Dad was just starting out. While at college in Bowling Green, Kentucky, a friend asked Dad to come to a college thing at his church. Dad wasn't interested until he learned that there would be girls there. Lots of girls. So he went to check it out.

Story goes that Mom saw him, went over and asked to share his hymnal. Halfway through the song Dad noticed that Mom knew all the words. They've been married for thirty-three years. I think sometimes we expect relationships to start like they do in the movies—and sometimes they do. My parents are evidence of that.

I know someone who really did meet her husband in the produce section of a grocery store. He noticed her amidst the grapes and bananas and stopped her in the parking lot to ask her out. People say it happens when you don't look for it to happen. I think this concept is comical because it causes people to "look" while appearing to be disinterested. If a person is aware in any way of the looking process, then she is looking. In fact, I'll go so far as to say that I don't know anyone who is single and not looking on some level. Not one person.

And that's it I think. We all listen to one another's stories and secretly plot, "Maybe that will work for me!" I guess I should ask a handsome stranger if I can share his hymnal. . . .

Love According to the Experts

• • • • • • • • • ANONYMOUS • • • • • • • • •

Kids from the ages of five to ten were asked questions about what they thought of love. Here are their interpretations of "happily ever after."

Falling in Love:

- "If falling in love is anything like learning how to spell, I don't want to do it. It takes too long." *(Glenn, age seven)*

- "Love is like an avalanche where you have to run for your life." *(John, age nine)*

- "I think you're supposed to get shot with an arrow or something, but the rest of it isn't supposed to be so painful." *(Manuel, age eight)*

- "No one is sure why it happens, but I heard it has something to do with how you smell. That's why perfume and deodorant are so popular." *(Mae, age nine)*

- "Love is the most important thing in the world, but baseball is pretty good too." *(Greg, age eight)*

- "Once I'm done with kindergarten, I'm going to find me a wife." *(Tom, age five)*

- "It gives me a headache to think about that stuff. I'm just a kid. I don't need that kind of trouble." *(Kenny, age seven)*

- "One of you should know how to write a check. Because, even if you have tons of love, there is still going to be a lot of bills." *(Ava, age eight)*

- "I'm not rushing into being in love. I'm finding fourth grade hard enough." *(Regina, age ten)*

- "A man and a woman promise to go through sickness and illness and diseases together." *(Marlon, age ten)*

- "[Being] single is better . . . for the simple reason that I wouldn't want to change no diapers. Of course, if I did get married, I'd figure something out. I'd just phone my mother and have her come over for some coffee and diaper changing." *(Kirsten, age ten)*

- "Love is foolish . . . but I still might try it sometime." *(Floyd, age nine)*

- "Love will find you, even if you are trying to hide from it. I been trying to hide from it since I was five, but the girls keep finding me." *(Dave, age eight)*

How People in Love Act:

- "Lovers will just be staring at each other and their food will get cold. Other people care more about the food." *(Brad, age eight)*

- "Romantic adults usually are all dressed up, so if they are just wearing jeans, it might mean they used to go out or they just broke up." *(Sarah, age nine)*

- "It's love if they order one of those desserts that is on fire. They like to order those because it's just like how their hearts are—on fire." *(Christine, age nine)*

- "See if the man picks up the check. That's how you can tell if he's in love." *(John, age nine)*
- "Many daters just eat pork chops and French fries and talk about love." *(Craig, age nine)*

Good Advice about Love:

- "Tell your wife that she looks pretty even if she looks like a truck!" *(Ricky, age seven)*
- "Sensitivity don't hurt." *(Robbie, age eight)*
- "Be a good kisser. It might make your wife forget that you never take out the trash." *(Erin, age eight)*
- "Don't say you love somebody and then change your mind. Love isn't like picking what movie you want to watch." *(Natalie, age nine)*

Why People in Love Often Hold Hands:

- "They want to make sure their rings don't fall off, because they paid good money for them." *(Gavin, age eight)*
- "They are just practicing for when they might have to walk down the aisle some day and do the holy matchimony thing." *(John, age nine)*

A Tempest in the School Teapot

• • • • • • • L. M. MONTGOMERY • • • • • • •

W hen Mr. Phillips was in the back of the room hearing Prissy Andrews's Latin, Diana whispered to Anne,

"That's Gilbert Blythe sitting right across the aisle from you, Anne. Just look at him and see if you don't think he's handsome."

Anne looked accordingly. She had a good chance to do so, for the said Gilbert Blythe was absorbed in stealthily pinning the long yellow braid of Ruby Gillis, who sat in front of him, to the back of her seat. He was a tall boy, with curly brown hair, roguish hazel eyes, and a mouth twisted into a teasing smile. Presently Ruby Gillis started up to take a sum to the master; she fell back into her seat with a little shriek, believing that her hair was pulled out by the roots. Everybody looked at her and Mr. Phillips glared so sternly that Ruby began to cry. Gilbert had whisked the pin out of sight and was studying his history with the soberest face in the world; but when the commotion subsided he looked at Anne and winked with inexpressible drollery.

"I think your Gilbert Blythe *is* handsome," confided Anne to Diana, "but I think he's very bold. It isn't good manners to wink at a strange girl."

But it was not until the afternoon that things really began to happen.

Mr. Phillips was back in the corner explaining a problem in

algebra to Prissy Andrews and the rest of the scholars were doing pretty much as they pleased eating green apples, whispering, drawing pictures on their slates, and driving crickets harnessed to strings, up and down the aisle. Gilbert Blythe was trying to make Anne Shirley look at him and failing utterly, because Anne was at that moment totally oblivious not only to the very existence of Gilbert Blythe, but of every other scholar in Avonlea school itself. With her chin propped on her hands and her eyes fixed on the blue glimpse of the Lake of Shining Waters that the west window afforded, she was far away in a gorgeous dreamland hearing and seeing nothing save her own wonderful visions.

Gilbert Blythe wasn't used to putting himself out to make a girl look at him and meeting with failure. She *should* look at him, that red-haired Shirley girl with the little pointed chin and the big eyes that weren't like the eyes of any other girl in Avonlea school.

Gilbert reached across the aisle, picked up the end of Anne's long red braid, held it out at arm's length and said in a piercing whisper:

"Carrots! Carrots!"

Then Anne looked at him with a vengeance!

She did more than look. She sprang to her feet, her bright fancies fallen into cureless ruin. She flashed one indignant glance at Gilbert from eyes whose angry sparkle was swiftly quenched in equally angry tears.

"You mean, hateful boy!" she exclaimed passionately. "How dare you!"

And then—thwack! Anne had brought her slate down on Gilbert's head and cracked it—slate not head—clear across.

Avonlea school always enjoyed a scene. This was an especially enjoyable one. Everybody said "Oh" in horrified delight. Diana gasped. Ruby Gillis, who was inclined to be hysterical, began to cry. Tommy Sloane let his team of crickets escape him altogether while he stared open-mouthed at the tableau.

Mr. Phillips stalked down the aisle and laid his hand heavily on Anne's shoulder.

"Anne Shirley, what does this mean?" he said angrily.

Anne returned no answer. It was asking too much of flesh and blood to expect her to tell before the whole school that she had been called "carrots." Gilbert it was who spoke up stoutly.

"It was my fault, Mr. Phillips. I teased her."

Mr. Phillips paid no heed to Gilbert.

"I am sorry to see a pupil of mine displaying such a temper and such a vindictive spirit," he said in a solemn tone, as if the mere fact of being a pupil of his ought to root out all evil passions from the hearts of small imperfect mortals. "Anne, go and stand on the platform in front of the blackboard for the rest of the afternoon."

Anne would have infinitely preferred a whipping to this punishment under which her sensitive spirit quivered as from a whiplash. With a white, set face she obeyed. Mr. Phillips took a chalk crayon and wrote on the blackboard above her head.

"Ann Shirley has a very bad temper. Ann Shirley must learn to control her temper," and then read it out loud so that even the primer class, who couldn't read writing, should understand it.

Anne stood there the rest of the afternoon with that legend above her. She did not cry or hang her head. Anger was still too hot in her heart for that and it sustained her amid all her agony of humiliation. With resentful eyes and passion-red cheeks she confronted alike Diana's sympathetic gaze and Charlie Sloane's indignant nods and Josie Pye's malicious smiles. As for Gilbert Blythe, she would not even look at him. She would *never* look at him again! She would never speak to him!!

The Bend in the Road

Halfway down the hill a tall lad came whistling out of a gate before the Blythe homestead. It was Gilbert, and the whistle died on his lips as he recognized Anne. He lifted his cap courteously, but he would have passed on in silence, if Anne had not stopped and held out her hand.

"Gilbert," she said, with scarlet cheeks, "I want to thank you for giving up the school for me. It was very good of you—and I want you to know that I appreciate it."

Gilbert took the offered hand eagerly.

"It wasn't particularly good of me at all, Anne. I was pleased to be able to do you some small service. Are we going to be friends after this? Have you really forgiven me my old fault?"

Anne laughed and tried unsuccessfully to withdraw her hand.

"I forgave you that day by the pond landing, although I didn't know it. What a stubborn little goose I was. I've been—I may as well make a complete confession—I've been sorry ever since."

"We are going to be the best of friends," said Gilbert, jubilantly. "We were born to be good friends, Anne. You've thwarted destiny enough. I know we can help each other in many ways. You are going to keep up your studies, aren't you? So am I. Come, I'm going to walk home with you."

Marilla looked curiously at Anne when the latter entered the kitchen.

"Who was that came up the lane with you, Anne?"

"Gilbert Blythe," answered Anne, vexed to find herself blushing. "I met him on Barry's hill."

"I didn't think you and Gilbert Blythe were such good friends that you'd stand for half an hour at the gate talking to him," said Marilla with a dry smile.

"We haven't been—we've been good enemies. But we have decided that it will be much more sensible to be good friends in the future. Were we really there half an hour? It seemed just a few minutes. But, you see, we have five years' lost conversations to catch up with, Marilla."

—from *Anne of Green Gables*

As Long as We Both Shall Live

• • • • • • • • • ANONYMOUS • • • • • • • • • •

A young man noticed that an elderly couple sitting down to lunch at McDonald's had ordered just one meal and an extra drink cup. As he watched, the gentleman carefully divided the hamburger in half then counted out the fries, one for him, one for her, until each had half of them. Next he poured half of the soft drink into the extra cup and set that in front of his wife. The old man then began to eat, and his wife sat watching, her hands folded demurely in her lap.

The young man decided to ask if they would allow him to purchase another meal for them so they didn't have to split theirs.

"Oh, no," the old gentleman replied. "We've been married fifty years, and everything has always been and will always be shared, fifty-fifty."

The young man then asked the wife if she was going to eat.

"Not yet," she replied. "It's his turn with the teeth."

The Baffling Question

• • • • • • • • • BILL COSBY • • • • • • • • • •

So you've decided to have a child. You've decided to give up quiet evenings with good books and lazy weekends with good music, intimate meals during which you finish whole sentences, sweet private times when you've savored the thought that just the two of you and your love are all you will ever need. You've decided to turn your sofas into trampolines, and to abandon the joys of leisurely contemplating reproductions of great art for the joys of frantically coping with reproductions of yourselves.

Why?

Poets have said the reason to have children is to give yourself immortality; and I must admit I did ask God to give me a son because I wanted someone to carry on the family name. Well, God did just that and I now confess that there have been times when I've told my son not to reveal who he is.

"You make up a name," I've said. "Just don't tell anybody who you are."

Immortality? Now that I have had five children, my only hope is that they all are out of the house before I die.

No, immortality was not the reason why my wife and I produced these beloved sources of dirty laundry and ceaseless noise. And we also did not have them because we thought it would be fun to see one of them sit in a chair and stick out his leg so that another one of them running by was launched like *Explorer I.* After which I said to the child who was the launching pad, "Why did you do that?"

"Do what?" he replied.

"Stick out your leg."

"Dad, I didn't know my leg was going out. My leg, it does that a lot."

If you cannot function in a world where things like this are said, then you better forget about raising children and go for daffodils.

My wife and I also did not have children so they could yell at each other all over the house, moving me to say, "What's the problem?"

"She's waving her foot in my room," my daughter replied.

"And something like that *bothers* you?"

"Yes, I don't *want* her foot in my room."

"Well," I said, dipping into my storehouse of paternal wisdom, "why don't you just close the door?"

"Then I can't see what she's doing!"

Furthermore, we did not have the children because we thought it would be rewarding to watch them do things that should be studied by the Menninger Clinic.

"Okay," I said to all five one day, "go get into the car."

All five then ran to the same car door, grabbed the same handle, and spent the next five minutes beating each other up. Not one of them had the intelligence to say, "Hey, *look.* There are three more doors." The dog, however, was already inside.

And we did not have the children to help my wife develop new lines for her face, or because she had always had a desire to talk out loud to herself: "Don't tell *me* you're *not* going to do something when I tell you to move!" And we didn't have children so I could always be saying to someone, "Where's my change?"

Like so many young couples, my wife and I simply were unable to project. In restaurants, we did not see the small children who were casting their bread on the water in the glasses the waiter had brought; and we did not see the mother who was fasting because she was both cutting the food for one child while pulling another from the floor to a chair that he would use for slipping to the floor again. And we did not project beyond those lovely Saturdays of buying precious little things after leisurely brunches together. We did not see that *other* precious little things would be coming along to destroy the first batch.

—from *Fatherhood*

Together Forever

Joey O'Connor

Every morning of your married life, you and your spouse will wake up and decide what you want to wear. If you're a guy, you will open the small military footlocker under your bed, which you received as a wedding gift. Say hello to your new horizontal closet. If you're lucky, someday you might get an armoire, but to find out what an armoire is, you'll have to look up that word in a French dictionary. (I didn't know what an armoire was until I got married; it wasn't on those marriage-preparation vocabulary tests.)

If you're a woman, you'll be delighted to know that you get the closet, the whole closet, and nothing but the closet, which is every newly married man's Nordstrom nightmare. Any remodeling you do in your master bedroom will be to increase the square footage of your closet. Why just last year, Krista and I built a two-thousand-square-foot addition to our master bedroom—a closet.

If your new husband is nice to you and brings you flowers every week, you may consider subletting a two-foot section of closet space to let him hang his shirts. Unless, of course, you're planning on buying him an armoire for his birthday. Forget those baseball season tickets; what your husband needs is a *manly armoire*. It's a guy thing. Definite *GQ* material.

—from *Have Your Wedding Cake and Eat It Too!*

A Male-Designed Curriculum for Training Wives

• • • • • • • BARBARA JOHNSON • • • • • • • •

1. *Silence, the Final Frontier:* Where No Woman Has Gone Before

2. *The Undiscovered Side of Banking:* Making Deposits

3. *Man Management:* Postponing Minor Household Chores 'til After the Game

4. *Bathroom Etiquette I:* Men Need Medicine Cabinet Space Too

5. *Bathroom Etiquette II:* His Razor Is His

6. *Communication Skills I:* Tears—the Last Resort, Not the First

7. *Communication Skills II:* Thinking Before Speaking

8. *Communication Skills III:* Getting What You Want Without Nagging

9. *Driving a Car Safely:* Introduction to Parking

10. *Telephone Skills 101:* How to Hang Up

11. *Water Retention:* Fact or Fat?

12. *Cooking I:* Bringing Back Bacon, Eggs, and Butter

13. *Advanced Cooking:* How Not to Inflict Your Diet on Other People

14. *PMS:* Your Problem . . . Not His

15. *Classic Clothing:* Wearing Outfits You Already Own
16. *Household Dust:* A Harmless Natural Occurrence Only Women Notice
17. *Integrating Your Laundry:* Washing It All Together
18. *Oil and Gas:* Your Car Needs *Both*
19. *TV Remotes:* For Men Only
20. *Shortening Your Attention Span:* How to Watch Fourteen TV Shows Simultaneously

—from *Leaking Laffs Between Pampers and Depends*

If Home Is Where the Heart Is—
Perhaps We Need a Bypass

KATHY PEEL

The greatest thing a mother can do for her children is love their father. And vice versa. For years this adage has been quoted, painted on plaques, and carved into paperweights. I for one believe there's some truth to this principle.

I don't want any recognition or awards, but let it be known that I try to love my husband and be a good wife. To do this, gracious person that I am, I've had to overlook a lot of things in my twenty-two-year marriage to Bill.

I've overlooked his climate eccentricities. When Bill ordered an electric blanket the night we checked into our honeymoon suite—the last day of July—I should have known what kind of life I was destined to lead. Frankly, I think all premarital counselors should administer a climate-compatibility test to every engaged couple. Forget the personality inventory tests that measure whether you're an introvert or an extrovert, passive or aggressive, and intuitive or pragmatic. This information is utterly useless when it comes to arguing over temperature. I think it's more important for a wife to understand from the beginning that her husband's feet turn to blocks of ice when the temperature goes below fifty. And a husband, on the other hand, would surely benefit from knowing his wife's idea of a cool breeze is North Dakota during a January Winnipeg Clipper gale.

Over the years we've learned to compromise. On the nights when Bill sets the thermostat to somewhere between *Some Like It Hot* and *Backdraft*, I simply open the windows. When I turn on the air conditioner in December and begin humming, "Let it snow, let it snow, let it snow," that's his cue to put on long underwear, turtleneck sweater, and wool socks.

I've also overlooked his recurring bad dreams about someone chasing and attacking him. Call me nonsensual, but my idea of intimate bedfellows is not being kicked in the midriff in the middle of the night. After his last bad dream, which of course he slept through like a baby, I woke him up.

"Excuse me," I tapped him on the shoulder, "but I didn't realize I was sleeping with Steven Seagal. Would you mind telling me who it is you're fighting off? I just want to know if it's worth my turning black and blue."

"Look," he replied, his eyes opened half-mast, "just cool your jets and be thankful you're not married to that guy I counseled last year who dreamed about water skiing. His wife's had back trouble ever since he used her as a slalom ski and made it twice around the lake. Go back to sleep."

And I've overlooked the ponderously slow way he makes decisions. I have never been your physically patient person. So when I ask Bill if he wants spaghetti for dinner and he has to mull it over, write out the pros and cons, check to see if it fits into his life blueprint, and pray about it, I start feeling a little testy. I decide it might be quicker to order in—from Sicily. Ask if he wants regular or creamy Italian dressing on his salad and I pull up a chair to get comfortable.

If we need to make a big decision—like buying a car—I prepare to grow old. I will never need a copy of *Consumer Reports*.

Bill methodically takes his time and collects answers to questions about cars the editors never dreamed of asking. The man becomes a walking automotive encyclopedia. On the other hand, when I think about buying a car, I only want to know two important facts: What color is it and will I look cute driving it?

Marriage is not expecting my husband, nor myself, to be perfect. It is cultivating flexibility, patience, understanding, and a sense of humor. It is our giving each other an atmosphere in which we can grow.

—from *The Stomach Virus and Other Forms*
of Family Bonding

To Keep Your Marriage Brimming

Ogden Nash

To keep your marriage brimming,
With love in the loving cup,
Whenever you're wrong admit it;
Whenever you're right shut up.

For Laughs . . .

The following are quotations that have been found in various church bulletins.

Church Bulletins

- ❀ "Thursday night potluck supper. Prayer and medication to follow."

- ❀ "Remember in prayer the many who are sick of our church and community."

- ❀ "O come all ye faithful, sin in exultation."

- ❀ "Bertha Belch, a missionary from Africa, will be speaking tonight at Calvary Memorial Church. Come tonight and hear Bertha Belch all the way from Africa."

- ❀ "Mr. Smith is also a close relative of his brother Wilbur in the church."

- ❀ "After today's service, coffee and donuts will be served in the basement. Please come down and say hell to the pastor."

- ❀ "Don't let worry kill you—let the church help."

- ❀ "For those of you who have children and don't know it, we have a nursery downstairs."

✤ "The rosebud on the altar this morning is to announce the birth of David Alan Belzer, the sin of Reverend and Mrs. Julius Belzer."

✤ "Children will be led in sinning and Bible study."

✤ "This afternoon there will be a meeting in the south and north ends of the church. Children will be baptized at both ends."

✤ "This being Easter Sunday, we will ask Mrs. Lewis to come forward and lay an egg on the altar."

✤ "There will be a baked bean supper next Sunday at 6:00 P.M. Music to follow."

✤ "At the evening service tonight, the sermon topic will be 'What is Hell?' Come early and listen to our choir practice."

✤ "Marriage: An Institution To Be Endured" —the subject of a sermon that should have read, "An Institution To Endure."

Part VI

When the Going Gets Tough . . . All Is Well

Laughter Is the Spice of Life in Adversity

A good laugh heals a lot of hurts.

—MADELEINE L'ENGLE

Trouble knocked on the door, but, hearing laughter, hurried away.

—BENJAMIN FRANKLIN

Man is the only animal that laughs and weeps; for he is the only animal that is struck with the difference between what things are, and what they ought to be.

—WILLIAM HENRY HAZLITT

Joy and Woe

WILLIAM BLAKE

It is right it should be so;
Man was made for joy and woe;
And when this we rightly know,
Through the world we safely go.
Joy and woe are woven fine,
A clothing for the soul divine;
Under every grief and pine
Runs a joy with silken twine.

—from "Auguries of Innocence"

Suffering Is Like Baking a Cake

• • • • • • • BARBARA JOHNSON • • • • • • •

I like to compare suffering to making a cake. No one sits down, gets out a box of baking powder, eats a big spoonful, and says, "Hmmm, that's good!" And you don't do that with a spoonful of shortening or raw eggs or flour, either. The tribulation and suffering in our lives can be compared with swallowing a spoonful of baking powder or shortening. By themselves these things are distasteful and they turn your stomach. But God takes all of these ingredients, stirs them up, and puts them in His own special oven, thinking *Surely the cake must be done by now*. But not yet, no, not yet. What really matters is that the cake is *baking* and the marvelous aroma is filling the house.

I find that people who trust God with their suffering have an invisible something, like the aroma of a freshly baked cake, that draws people to them. As Paul put it, "All things [all the ingredients of pain and suffering] work together for good to them that love God" (Rom. 8:28 KJV).

When we believe that nothing comes to us except through our heavenly Father, then suffering begins to make a little sense to us—not much, I admit, but a little bit, and that's all God needs to work in our lives, just a mustard seed of faith. Then we can see that God is using our pain to work something in us that is redemptive. Every trial or broken relationship goes into God's oven and eventually we begin to "smell" like cake or fresh bread. Even our suffering counts for something!

—from *Pack Up Your Gloomees in a Great Big Box,*
Then Sit on the Lid and Laugh!

A New Departure in Flavorings

• • • • • • • L. M. MONTGOMERY • • • • • • •

Monday and Tuesday great preparations went on at Green Gables. Having the minister and his wife to tea was a serious and important undertaking, and Marilla was determined not to be eclipsed by any of the Avonlea housekeepers. Anne was wild with excitement and delight. She talked it all over with Diana Tuesday night in the twilight, as they sat on the big red stones by the Dryad's Bubble and made rainbows in the water with little twigs dipped in fir balsam.

"Everything is ready, Diana, except my cake which I'm to make in the morning, and the baking-powder biscuits which Marilla will make just before teatime. I assure you, Diana, that Marilla and I have had a busy two days of it. It's such a responsibility having a minister's family to tea. I never went through such an experience before. You should just see our pantry. It's a sight to behold. We're going to have jellied chicken and cold tongue. We're to have two kinds of jelly, red and yellow, and whipped cream and lemon pie, and cherry pie, and three kinds of cookies, and fruit cake, and Marilla's famous yellow plum preserves that she keeps especially for ministers, and pound cake and layer cake, and biscuits as aforesaid; and new bread and old both, in case the minister is dyspeptic and can't eat new. Mrs. Lynde says ministers are dyspeptic, but I don't think Mr. Allan has been a minister long enough for it to have had a bad effect on him. I just grow cold when I think of my layer cake. Oh, Diana, what if it shouldn't be good! I dreamed last night that I was chased all around by a fearful goblin with a big layer cake for a head."

"It'll be good, all right," assured Diana, who was a very comfortable sort of friend. "I'm sure that piece of the one you made that we had for lunch in Idlewild two weeks ago was perfectly elegant."

"Yes; but cakes have such a terrible habit of turning out bad just when you especially want them to be good," sighed Anne, setting a particularly well-balsamed twig afloat. "However, I suppose I shall just have to trust to Providence and be careful to put in the flour."

Wednesday morning came. Anne got up at sunrise because she was too excited to sleep. She had caught a severe cold in the head by reason of her dabbling in the spring on the preceding evening, but nothing short of absolute pneumonia could have quenched her interest in culinary matters that morning. After breakfast she proceeded to make her cake. When she finally shut the oven door upon it she drew a long breath.

"I'm sure I haven't forgotten anything this time, Marilla. But do you think it will rise? Just suppose perhaps the baking powder isn't good? I used it out of the new can. And Mrs. Lynde says you can never be sure of getting good baking powder nowadays when everything is so adulterated. Mrs. Lynde says the government ought to take the matter up, but she says we'll never see the day when a Tory government will do it. Marilla, what if that cake doesn't rise?"

"We'll have plenty without it" was Marilla's unimpassioned way of looking at the subject.

The cake did rise, however, and came out of the oven as light and feathery as golden foam. Anne, flushed with delight, clapped it together with layers of ruby jelly and, in imagination, saw Mrs. Allan eating it and possibly asking for another piece! . . .

Anne laid herself out to decorate in a manner and after a fashion that should leave Mrs. Barry's nowhere. Having abundance of roses and ferns and a very artistic taste of her own, she made that tea table such a thing of beauty that when the minister and his wife sat down to it they exclaimed in chorus over its loveliness.

"It's Anne's doings," said Marilla, grimly just; and Anne felt that Mrs. Allan's approving smile was almost too much happiness for this world. . . .

All went merry as a marriage bell until Anne's layer cake was passed. Mrs. Allan, having already been helped to a bewildering variety, declined it. But Marilla, seeing the disappointment on Anne's face, said smilingly:

"Oh, you must take a piece of this, Mrs. Allan. Anne made it on purpose for you."

"In that case I must sample it," laughed Mrs. Allan, helping herself to a plump triangle, as did also the minister and Marilla.

Mrs. Allan took a mouthful of hers and a most peculiar expression crossed her face; not a word did she say, however, but steadily ate away at it. Marilla saw the expression and hastened to taste the cake.

"Anne Shirley!" she exclaimed. "What on earth did you put into that cake?"

"Nothing but what the recipe said, Marilla," cried Anne with a look of anguish. "Oh, isn't it all right?"

"All right! It's simply horrible. Mr. Allan, don't try to eat it. Anne, taste it yourself. What flavoring did you use?"

"Vanilla," said Anne, her face scarlet with mortification after tasting the cake. "Only vanilla. Oh, Marilla, it must have been the baking powder. I had my suspicions of that bak—"

"Baking powder fiddlesticks! Go and bring me the bottle of vanilla you used."

Anne fled to the pantry and returned with a small bottle partially filled with a brown liquid and labeled yellowly, "Best Vanilla."

Marilla took it, uncorked it, smelled it.

"Mercy on us, Anne, you've flavored that cake with *anodyne liniment.* I broke the liniment bottle last week and poured what was left into an old empty vanilla bottle. I suppose it's partly my fault—I should have warned you—but for pity's sake, why couldn't you have smelled it?"

Anne dissolved into tears under this double disgrace.

"I couldn't—I had such a cold!" and with this she fairly fled to the gable chamber, where she cast herself on the bed and wept as one who refuses to be comforted.

Presently a light step sounded on the stairs and somebody entered the room.

"Oh, Marilla," sobbed Anne, without looking up, "I'm disgraced forever. I shall never be able to live this down. It will get out—things always do get out in Avonlea. Diana will ask me how my cake turned out and I shall have to tell her the truth. I shall always be pointed at as the girl who flavored a cake with anodyne liniment. Gil—the boys in school will never get over laughing at it. Oh, Marilla, if you have a spark of Christian pity don't tell me that I must go down and wash the dishes after this. I'll wash them when the minister and his wife are gone, but I cannot ever look Mrs. Allan in the face again. Perhaps she'll think I tried to poison her. Mrs. Lynde says she knows an orphan girl who tried to poison her benefactor. But the liniment isn't poisonous. It's meant to be taken internally—although not in cakes. Won't you tell Mrs. Allan so, Marilla?"

"Suppose you jump up and tell her so yourself," said a merry voice.

Anne flew up, to find Mrs. Allan standing by her bed, surveying her with laughing eyes.

"My dear little girl, you mustn't cry like this," she said, genuinely disturbed by Anne's tragic face. "Why, it's all just a funny mistake that anybody might make."

"Oh, no, it takes me to make such a mistake," said Anne forlornly. "And I wanted to have that cake so nice for you, Mrs. Allan."

"Yes, I know, dear. And I assure you I appreciate your kindness and thoughtfulness just as much as if it had turned out all right. Now, you mustn't cry any more, but come down with me and show me your flower garden. Miss Cuthbert tells me you have a little plot all your own. I want to see it, for I'm very much interested in flowers."

Anne permitted herself to be led down and comforted, reflecting that it was really providential that Mrs. Allan was a kindred spirit. Nothing more was said about the liniment cake, and when the guests went away Anne found that she had enjoyed the evening more than could have been expected, considering that terrible incident. Nevertheless, she sighed deeply.

"Marilla, isn't it nice to think that tomorrow is a new day with no mistakes in it yet?"

"I'll warrant you'll make plenty in it," said Marilla. "I never saw your beat for making mistakes, Anne."

"Yes, and well I know it," admitted Anne mournfully. "But have you ever noticed one encouraging thing about me, Marilla? I never make the same mistake twice."

"I don't know as that's much benefit when you're always making new ones."

"Oh, don't you see, Marilla? There must be a limit to the mistakes one person can make, and when I get to the end of them, then I'll be through with them. That's a very comforting thought."

"Well, you'd better go and give that cake to the pigs," said Marilla. "It isn't fit for any human to eat. . . ."

—from *Anne of Green Gables*

Choosing Joy

. . . . MARILYN MEBERG . . . .

Y ou may feel there are times in life that simply will not yield even an ounce of humor. May I suggest that during those seemingly interminable times of pain, you fight to see beyond the restrictive confines of the immediate; remind yourself that those moments will not last forever. Whatever it is that threatens to crush your spirit and claim your joy today will not necessarily be there tomorrow, next month, or next year. Life moves forward and circumstances change. You will not always be in a pit! That reminder in itself brings a respite to the soul. From there perhaps a glimmer of light can seep through the darkness, enabling you to search out that seemingly elusive but spirit-lifting smile or laugh that helps you regain control. . . .

Ephesians 1:11 reminds us that God, in His sovereign love and power "works all things after the counsel of His will." My security, my rest, my peace, and my joy live always in the secure knowledge of that comforting truth. But God invites my participation in the executing of His divine will for my life. To me, a part of that participation has to do with how I perceive the events of my life. I determine whether or not I'm going to view my experiences through a negative or a positive lens. If indeed my perceptions are negative, then it stands to reason my life will feel out of whack, and . . . I can spend years pouting in my cave. Thank

God I don't have to pout, fuss, or complain; I have the option to smile, chuckle, or laugh. When I do, in that arena where God invites my participation, I am in control. . . .

What greater testimony can we give an unbelieving world than a cheerful, joyful demeanor that bespeaks an unshakable faith in the provision of an almighty God? . . . Cheerfulness and joy are not moral requirements for Christian living, but I do believe they are a consequence, an inevitable result, of our faith in God. When we attempt to generate joy within ourselves apart from God, it is sporadic at best. Ultimately, we sense the inability and depletedness of our own humanity.

Living in response to the abundance of God is simply having the faith to rest in His provision and to believe in His individual caring. The familiar Philippians 4:19 passage states, "My God shall supply all your need according to His riches in glory in Christ Jesus." These are joy-producing scriptural reminders. They can strengthen our faith because when our faith is strengthened, our joy returns. When our joy returns, so does our smile. That smile then becomes a positive witness to the reality of our faith. . . .

[W]e as believers in Christ, who conquered death, have the last laugh. As we walk through this life, we encounter pain, we encounter heartache, and we encounter sorrow. But at the end of it all, we encounter God! The last laugh is ours!

—from *Choosing the Amusing*

A Matter of Perspective

BARBARA JOHNSON

One of the people I admire most when it comes to laughing in the face of misery is my friend Joni Eareckson Tada. What a gift she has for bringing joy into the most trying situations! Paralyzed in a diving accident, Joni has spent the last thirty-plus years in a motorized wheelchair. She writes inspiring books, paints beautiful pictures, and heads a ministry called Joni and Friends, which focuses on inspiring, helping, and sharing God's love with other wheelchair-bound Christians around the world.

Thank heaven Joni was with us at a California venue when another "misadventure"—actually quite a serious problem—occurred during a Women of Faith conference. Somehow a misunderstanding had occurred, and the conference was seriously oversold. As a result, hundreds of women showed up to attend the conference—and found *other* women already sitting in their assigned seats—and holding ticket stubs to prove they were right! The conference coordinators put out a frantic call for chairs and eventually managed to borrow some narrow, hard folding chairs from a funeral home. The seats were hastily arranged in a dark basement area of the arena, and television monitors were wheeled in so the women could see—if they had really good eyes!

As you might imagine, there were quite a few impatient and disgruntled women in that crowded room! After all, they had bought tickets like everyone else, and there they sat on those cold, hard chairs. They were still muttering when the lights were dimmed and the program began. The women in the little folding chairs leaned forward, squinting to see the monitors. Joni was the first main speaker. As she sat peacefully in her wheelchair, the tiny elevator beside the stage silently lifted her up to the platform. She motored out to the center of the stage and smiled into the cameras, greeting the thousands of listeners with her melodic alto voice.

"I hear that some of you aren't too happy with your chairs tonight," she said with a warm smile. She slowly rotated her wheelchair so she could look out at the audience all the way around her. "I certainly understand your feelings," she continued, her smile never waning. "I *hate* my chair!"

There was a little collective gasp from the audience as Joni's words sank in while all eyes took in the sight of her frail, slim body strapped into the wheelchair. "And you know what?" Joni asked, her eyes twinkling merrily. "I have a thousand friends who would *gladly* change chairs with you right now!"

Suddenly the tension was eased in the vast auditorium—and in the dark, cramped basement—and twenty thousand women had a new perspective on the evening.

—from *Leaking Laffs Between Pampers and Depends*

Happily Ever After

NICOLE JOHNSON

You don't find hope; it finds you. But hope is a double-edged sword. While it's elevating and inspiring, after a few too many disappointments, we aren't so sure we want our hopes raised anymore. When the fairy tales stir up hope, and our hungry hearts respond, if life doesn't come through, we get out of sorts with hope. Perhaps we're even angry with the fairy tales for letting us down. We missed the ending we wanted. Where was the detour sign? Snow White to the left—Black Misery to the right? No one gave us a choice. It would have been better never to hope for anything.

Have you given up on hope? Try taking this little quiz to discover the shade of your jade:

Happily ever after is a myth . . .

_____ Only during my period.

_____ Almost every day.

_____ Since 1941.

Someday my prince will come . . .

_____ About 5:30, after work.

_____ He got lost on the way and wouldn't ask for directions.

_____ Yep, he came, and now he's in the other room, watching TV.

If there were a glass slipper . . .

_____ I would try it on for fun.

_____ I would assume it doesn't come in my size.

_____ I would fill it with rocks and plants and make a terrarium.

My biggest dream is . . .

_____ A richer life.

_____ More money than bills.

_____ A good night's sleep.

If seven dwarfs showed up on my doorstep, I might . . .

_____ Invite them in for tea.

_____ Act like I don't speak English.

_____Call the exterminator.

(Hint: if you chose the last option every time, please keep reading.) . . .

Many of our dreams will not be completed just yet. But it would make me far sadder to think that there was no hope or dream or prayer that they ever would be completed or fulfilled. We may not get it all in this lifetime. Many of our longings will only be answered and fulfilled in heaven, but that still gives us hope. A day is coming when we will walk free. One day we will be given the desires of our hearts, and our prayers will be answered. So we wait in the hope that God will bring all things to completion, knowing that the greatest and certainly the most lasting completions are yet to come. For only heaven can satisfy and fulfill the deepest desires of our hearts.

—from _Keeping a Princess Heart in a Not-So-Fairy-Tale World_

Looking Forward

· · · · · · · · Mark Lowry · · · · · · · ·

I've spent most of my life looking forward. I look forward to Thanksgiving (in spite of football), when I'm home with my family sitting around my mother's 5'x16' dining-room table, eating that bountiful feast. (She can seat about sixteen people at that table, and every Thanksgiving it's usually full. You've got to make reservations a year in advance, even if you're one of her kids.)

I look forward to my birthday. Well, I used to. I'm starting to actually dread it because it comes too often. It used to mosey around once a year, but now it seems to come every six months.

I usually have more fun looking forward to something than actually doing it.

I spend two months looking forward to Thanksgiving, and then the turkey may be dry, and someone has the *audacity* to make bread dressing instead of cornbread dressing! I start looking forward to Christmas shopping the day following Thanksgiving and spend a lot of time buying presents and having them wrapped. Then, with a flick of the wrist, the wrapping paper falls to the floor, and the recipients scream, "Oh, my, it's just what we *wanted!*" Then they take them back the following day to get what they *really* wanted.

And it's the day *after* Christmas.

Again.

Looking forward to things is great.

But the memories can be greater.

My grandfather spent the last two years of his life in a nursing home. He had a stroke. He was the greatest Paw Paw a kid could have. But Paw Paw couldn't remember very well toward the end. Mama would visit him in the morning, and when she'd come back in the afternoon, he couldn't remember that she'd been there that morning.

But Paw Paw could remember yesteryear. He remembered working for Humble Oil Company, which is now Exxon. He remembered working for a sheet-metal company in Houston. He could remember the church's Sunday dinners on the ground and his years singing in the male quartet.

But the last years of his life he just sat in his wheelchair looking forward to the Lord coming back. He looked forward to a day when memories and plans are one and the same. There's no night there, and time is a thing of the past. And I'm sure, over the door of heaven there must be a sign that reads: NO WHEELCHAIRS, HOSPITAL BEDS, OR BEDPANS ALLOWED!

It doesn't take much to excite me. I look forward to getting new things—new clothes, a new car, a new home. But those days were over for Paw Paw. He had many reasons to look forward to heaven. His wheelchair will not be needed, his hospital bed will be history, and his mind will be brand-new.

He looked forward to going "home." And I'd rarely see him without a smile on his face, because he knew where he was going.

I've always said there's no fear in graduating from high school if you know where you're going. There's no fear in graduating from college if you know where you're going. So I guess there's no fear in dying if you know where you're going.

I've seen it in Paw Paw's eyes. I've seen it in his smile. He knew where he was going.

Because there was one memory he never forgot: the day the preacher came by his house at 911 Prince Drive in Houston and led him to Christ.

The best way to become Paw Paw's age and have wonderful memories is to live a life with heaven in mind, to always know where you're going.

—from *Out of Control*

Finding the Amusing

. . . . ANNE FRANK . . . .

I have often been downcast, but never in despair; I regard our hiding as a dangerous adventure, romantic and interesting at the same time. In my diary I treat all the privations as amusing. I have made up my mind now to lead a different life from other girls and, later on, different from ordinary housewives. My start has been so very full of interest, and that is the sole reason why I have to laugh at the humorous side of the most dangerous moments.

—from *The Diary of Anne Frank*

We Can Laugh . . . Now

JONI EARECKSON TADA • • • • • • •

Did we see God work miracles on this trip, or *what!*" I smiled to Judy as we boarded our plane home. It had been a grand weekend of ministry, reminding me once again of the joy of serving Jesus.

Then our plane landed. It hadn't been the best of flights, but we were glad to be back. Then we sat curbside at the airport, our smiles fading as we kept checking our watches—the handicap *Super Shuttle* never did turn up. After an hour of heat, car fumes, yelling cops, and honking horns, Judy hailed a cab, jammed in our luggage, and enlisted the reluctant cab driver's help to transfer me into the front seat. We chugged away from the curb and—clunk! The engine died.

Our driver abandoned us to find help, while impatient motorists screeched by shaking their fists. Judy tried to squirm past the luggage in the back seat to open my passenger door, but she was stuck. We were helpless to do anything but wait.

After a police officer jump-started the cab, we proceeded up the San Diego freeway, crawling at twenty-five miles per hour. It was rush hour. "Whaat eez dis terrible traffick!" our Iranian cab driver yelled, waving his hand in disgust. I eyed the ticker chocking up miles . . . and money.

An hour and a half later, we pulled up to my driveway. How I longed for Ken to be home to greet us, but he was away fishing. I missed him. And I missed him even more when Judy realized that, between us, we didn't have enough cash for the enormous cab fare. "No checks, lady," our driver shook his head. "No credit cards, either."

Judy hurried to the front door, turned the key, and—brrrring!— the house alarm went off. I had given her the wrong code! Exasperated, she fumbled with the alarm buttons, opened the door, and let me in. I assured her I'd be okay by myself until she came back—the cab driver had to take her to Ralph's Market so she could cash a check to pay him. My nerves were raw, my back was aching, and I was exhausted from the three-hour time change. As I began to power my wheelchair through the house, suddenly—brrrring!—I had tripped the motion sensor. When I wheeled to the control panel to punch the off button, I burst into tears: my paralyzed hands could only flop against the panel, striking even more buttons. My head was pounding . . . but . . . it wasn't my head . . . it was the front door—Judy had failed to abort the silent alarm to the police station. It was the Calabasas cops. "I'm sorry," I screamed above the alarm, "I can't open the door!" They replied, but I couldn't hear them—the telephone was ringing.

Finally Judy returned. The cops left and the cab left. She slumped against the front door . . . and we cried. No, we laughed. Then we cried some more. "Well, it *was* a great ministry week-end," we consoled each other, at which point we started laughing again.

I shouldn't be surprised at trials like these, especially on the heels of a fantastic ministry trip. I'd like to describe kaput engines and tripped alarms as tricks of the devil, but in fact they are simply a dead engine and a perfectly-working house alarm. It's part of the territory that comes with serving Jesus. Christian service includes the ordinary, earthly challenges.

If we're going to stand up and make a difference for Christ, while others lounge about, you can be sure we'll encounter hardships, obstacles, nuisances, hassles, and inconveniences—much more than the average couch potato. And we shouldn't be surprised. Such difficulty while serving Christ isn't necessarily suffering—it's status quo.

—from *Holiness in Hidden Places*

Consider God's Care

PATSY CLAIRMONT

You're not going to believe this, but honest, this story is true. (I promise you my prize, 1940s Shirley Temple paper dolls if it isn't!) A relative of my friend Bev unexpectedly moved into Bev's home for a lengthy stay.

Okay, that's disruptive, but not unbelievable, you say? Just wait.

This relative, whom we'll call Gwenda, came with baggage. Not just with luggage but with her pets in tow. Yes, pets, plural. A dog, Bertha, dubbed for her gargantuan size and a wiry chicken named Weezer.

Don't check your hearing aid; you heard right, a cotton-pickin' chicken. Now I have a lot of friends who own pet birds, but a chicken? Just hearing that a fowl moved into Bev's house ruffled my feathers. Fortunately, Weezer showed up in a cage. I know this because Bev decided shortly after Weezer's arrival to change the newspapers in the tray (for obvious reasons). Bev grabbed up the comic strips and quickly lined the bottom of the cage, thinking what a sacrificial effort she was making. A little while later Gwenda strolled by, spotted the comics, and hit the roof. Seems Weezer doesn't have a sense of humor because she only likes the black and white sections of the newspaper. No, I'm not making this up. The funnies are not funny to Weezer.

So Bev pulled out the "Family Circus" and replaced it with the obituaries. Weezer nestled right in.

And get this: Weezer loves lettuce, but it has to be heated first. I wonder how Gwenda figured that out. Maybe Weezer pecked out a message like Morse Code. "Gwenda, for heaven's sake, heat the lettuce!"

Anyway, Gwenda frequents Bev's already congested kitchen, skillet in hand, sautéing Weezer's gourmet meals. (I have a feeling the hostess would like to sauté . . . well, never mind.) Weezer is no dumb cluck. This chick knows which side her lettuce is heated on.

Speaking of heat, Weezer's home state of Florida, known for its warm days, annoys Weezer's sensitivies; so Gwenda keeps a fan running for her chickette. I can hear Weezer now: "A little to the right . . . now a little to the left . . . ahh, that's better." Talk about ruffled feathers. Can you picture a fanned chicken—feathers parted, head plastered against the bars, wings pulsating in time to the whir?

If you're thinking about adopting the Weezer clan, know that your electric bill will grow. Seems when you go out for the evening, Weezer gets scared if left in the dark, so you'll need to leave on the lights.

And if you're thinking it won't matter, then know that big Bertha becomes frantic when her chicken friend isn't happy and tends to leave little droplets around the house. Actually, nothing big Bertha leaves could be described as little. (Did I mention Bertha would only drink water from a Starbucks coffee mug?)

Life is definitely funnier than fiction. And a neurotic chicken makes me cluck. Of course, I can guffaw because Weezer is hundreds of miles away from me. If this group were my houseguests, why, the solution seems simple. I'd send Weezer, Bertha, and their keeper to a faraway farm, perhaps to a funny farm. There Weezer could possibly develop a sense of humor. Then I'd call Kentucky Fried Chicken; that way Weezer could have a last laugh. Run, chicken, run! . . .

[W]e probably won't want to go out and buy a Weezer, but we may want to consider the ravens . . . oh, not for purchase, but for winged thoughts to ponder.

Ravens are scavenger birds, the pirates of the air, out looking for a meal. But here's the impressive part: God provides it. Sometimes, not always, but sometimes, those we take in are our guests by God's design. He is using us and them for more reasons than we understand. That's where inconvenience becomes relinquishment, and relinquishment leads to a more expansive heart for us all.

So if Aunt Gwenda knocks with Bertha at her side and Weezer tucked under her arm, before we send them off to the farm, realize they may be God's ravens.

—from *The Hat Box*

Accepting the Detours

• • • • • • • • • LUCI SWINDOLL • • • • • • • • •

During a Women of Faith conference in Denver recently, a tiny mouse got on the porch where the speakers sit. Who knows how it got there? Perhaps it was fond of worship music and wanted to enjoy our singing up close and personal. I wish you could have seen the reaction of my porch pals when that little mouse showed up. Thelma shrieked, stuck her legs straight out in front of her and hid behind her purple purse the size of Kansas; Patsy sat on both legs until they disappeared; Sheila screamed bloody murder but didn't have to levitate since she spends her life on four-inch heels anyway; and Marilyn looked at the thing, kicked it aside, and turned to me with, "I'll bet that mouse is scared to death of all these women."

I chided the whole bunch with a characteristically loving comment: "Roaches in Africa are bigger than this little varmint. Get a grip." And we all went right back to singing "All Things Are Possible." (Fortunately, none of the eighteen thousand women in the audience knew what was happening or it wouldn't have been the mouse that roared.)

In life, we have no way of knowing what's going to happen next. And, we never know for sure how we'll respond. We often plan one thing and, on the way, experience another that's even more interesting, meaningful, or unusual. Our journeys through life are regularly interrupted by detours from the intended course. On an average day, who can predict what might happen? A friend stops by with staggering news. An uninvited mouse unexpectedly scurries across our path. We win a trip to Bora Bora. What do we do now?

A couple of years ago Marilyn Meberg and I spoke on Mackinac Island, off the coast of Michigan. We got stranded due to bad weather. In order to catch our plane on time, we had to take a horse and buggy, boat, taxi, and bus. Literally! At every juncture it seemed one more thing went wrong. We might have worried ourselves into a very bad mood or complained and made our displeasure known to all who crossed our path. We could have had a miserable day. We certainly had all the ingredients to make us out of sorts. But we were together; and there was absolutely nothing we could do to improve our lot in life, for that day anyway. So we decided to make the most of the adventure. Having made such a good decision as that, we had the time of our lives. We've looked back on that day as one of the most memorable times of spontaneous fun we've ever enjoyed in our long friendship.

All along the way during that very unpredictable day, we played a ridiculous game. "Hey, Mare," I said, "they say we'll miss the boat because of the fog, but I don't think we will. I'll buy you breakfast if we do." She came back with a snappy retort: "You little optimist. Of course we'll miss the boat. If we don't, break-fast is on me." She bought breakfast.

Later, it was obvious the taxi would not be waiting in the desig-nated spot. "Hey, Mare," I said, "they say we'll arrive too late to catch the bus, but I don't think we will. I'll buy you lunch if we do." Marilyn responded, "You silly girl. Of course we're going to miss the bus. Look at your watch. If we don't, lunch is on me." She bought lunch.

And so the day went just like that. We were in a pickle for sure. But somehow, our experience was delightful. In the end, we got home without a hitch. I was very full and Marilyn, very poor. She'd picked up the tab for all three meals and every snack. Actually, it was very cheap entertainment for us both. And we laughed ourselves silly.

It's all in the attitude. Once we learn to capture these unexpected moments of surprise and potential disappointment, an even greater spirit of adventure is born in our hearts.

—from *I Married Adventure*

Then our mouth was filled with laughter,
And our tongue with singing.
Then they said among the nations,
"The LORD has done great things for them."
The LORD has done great things for us,
And we are glad.
(Psalm 126:2–3)

Acknowledgments

G rateful acknowledgment is made to the publishers and copyright holders who granted permission to reprint copyrighted material. In a few cases, it was not possible to trace the original authors. The compilers will be happy to rectify this if and when the authors contact them by writing to W Publishing Group, 402 BNA Drive, Building 100, Suite 600, Nashville, TN 37217.

Part I: A Laugh Is a Smile That Bursts

"Choosing Happiness" by Andy Andrews. Reprinted by permission of Thomas Nelson, Inc., Nashville, Tennessee, from the book entitled *The Traveler's Gift*, copyright date 2002 by Andy Andrews. All rights reserved.

"Laugh" by Nicole Johnson. Reprinted by permission. *Fresh-Brewed Life*, Nicole Johnson, copyright date 1999, W Publishing, Nashville, Tennessee. All rights reserved.

"A Formula for Laughter" by Marilyn Meberg. Reprinted by permission. *I'd Rather Be Laughing*, Marilyn Meberg, copyright date 1998, W Publishing, Nashville, Tennessee. All rights reserved.

"Playful Pleasures" by Luci Swindoll. Reprinted by permission. *The Great Adventure*, Patsy Clairmont, Barbara Johnson, Marilyn Meberg, Luci Swindoll, Sheila Walsh, and Thelma Wells, copyright date 2002, W Publishing, Nashville, Tennessee. All rights reserved.

Part II: Mama Knows Best

Part III: Whistle While You Work

Part IV: Fit to Be Tied

Meberg, Luci Swindoll, Sheila Walsh, and Thelma Wells, copyright date 2002, W Publishing, Nashville, Tennessee. All rights reserved.

"Release the Tension" by JoAnna Harris. Copyright © 2004. Used by permission. www.joannaharris.com

"Household Management for an Unmanageable Person" by Kathy Peel. Reprinted by permission. *Do Plastic Surgeons Take Visa? and Other Confessions of a Desperate Woman,* Kathy Peel, copyright date 1992, W Publishing, Nashville, Tennessee. All rights reserved.

"Celebrating Imagination" by Luci Swindoll. Reprinted by permission. *You Bring the Confetti, God Brings the Joy,* Luci Swindoll, copyright date 1986, W Publishing, Nashville, Tennessee. All rights reserved.

"Exercise Advice" by Mark Lowry. Reprinted by permission. *Out of Control,* Mark Lowry, copyright date 1996, W Publishing, Nashville, Tennessee. All rights reserved.

"The Truth About Dentists" by Lewis Grizzard. From *Won't You Come Home, Billy Bob Bailey?* by Lewis Grizzard. © 1980 by Lewis Grizzard. Reprinted by permission of Peachtree Publishers, Ltd.

"How Can I Be Over the Hill When I Never Even Got to the Top?" by Barbara Johnson. Reprinted by permission. *Splashes of Joy in the Cesspools of Life,* Barbara Johnson, copyright date 1992, W Publishing, Nashville, Tennessee. All rights reserved.

"Chasing Pots" by Thelma Wells. Reprinted by permission. *The Great Adventure,* Patsy Clairmont, Barbara Johnson, Marilyn Meberg, Luci Swindoll, Sheila Walsh, and Thelma Wells, copyright date 2002, W Publishing, Nashville, Tennessee. All rights reserved.

"Life Is a Beautiful Thing" by Luci Swindoll. Reprinted by permission. *You Bring the Confetti, God Brings the Joy,* Luci

Part V: Till Death (or Insanity) Do Us Part

Part VI: When the Going Gets Tough . . . All Is Well

"Suffering Is Like Baking a Cake" by Barbara Johnson. Reprinted by permission. *Pack Up Your Gloomees in a Great Big Box, Then Sit on the Lid and Laugh!* Barbara Johnson, copyright date 1993, W Publishing, Nashville, Tennessee. All rights reserved.

"Choosing Joy" by Marilyn Meberg. Reprinted by permission. *Choosing the Amusing,* Marilyn Meberg, copyright date 1999, W Publishing, Nashville, Tennessee. All rights reserved.

"A Matter of Perspective" by Barbara Johnson. Reprinted by permission. *Leaking Laffs Between Pampers and Depends,* Barbara Johnson, copyright date 2000, W Publishing, Nashville, Tennessee. All rights reserved.

"Happily Ever After" by Nicole Johnson. Reprinted by permission. *Keeping a Princess Heart in a Not-So-Fairy-Tale World,* Nicole Johnson, copyright date 2003, W Publishing, Nashville, Tennessee. All rights reserved.

"Looking Forward" by Mark Lowry. Reprinted by permission. *Out of Control,* Mark Lowry, copyright date 1996, W Publishing, Nashville, Tennessee. All rights reserved.

"We Can Laugh . . . Now" by Joni Eareckson Tada. Reprinted by permission. *Holiness in Hidden Places,* Joni Eareckson Tada, copyright date 1999, J. Countryman, Nashville, Tennessee. All rights reserved.

"Consider God's Care" by Patsy Clairmont. Reprinted by permission. *The Hat Box,* Patsy Clairmont, copyright date 2003, W Publishing, Nashville, Tennessee. All rights reserved.

"Accepting the Detours" by Luci Swindoll. Reprinted by permission. *I Married Adventure,* Luci Swindoll, copyright date 2002, W Publishing, Nashville, Tennessee. All rights reserved.

Also Available from

WOMEN OF FAITH®

Irrepressible Hope
Devotions to Anchor Your Soul and
Buoy Your Spirit

Hope is the unbreakable spiritual lifeline that connects us straight into the heart of God. In this dynamic sixty-day devotional, the Women of Faith speakers identify the emotions that come from a life void of hope and direct us to the source of all hope—Christ. What better remedy for a troubled world than to offer huge doses of Irrepressible Hope?

The Great Adventure
A Devotional Journey of the Heart,
Soul, and Mind

These sixty devotionals by the six Women of Faith speakers will serve as a guide and encouragement for women who are in the journey of life. With their contagious wit and wisdom, they will soon have the reader embracing the adventure of life through learning how to trust God with all things.

The Women of Faith® Devotional Bible

A Message of Grace and Hope for Every Day

The Women of Faith® Devotional Bible provides women with the inspiration and resources needed to strengthen their walk with God and build stronger relationships with others. It helps women of all ages and stages in life—mature believers and those who have yet to believe, from all backgrounds, church and non-churched—to grow spiritually, emotionally, and relationally.

Writers of the devotionals include the well-known Women of Faith® speakers: Patsy Clairmont, Barbara Johnson, Marilyn Meberg, Luci Swindoll, Sheila Walsh, and Thelma Wells.

Contributing writers include: Kathy Troccoli, Jan Silvious, Jill Briscoe, Babbie Mason, Point of Grace, and many others.

Women of Faith® Study Guide Series

These topical guides will deal with issues that women wrestle with today: God's Will, Living in Christ, Prayer, and Worry.

Reaching an audience across race, socioeconomic, denominational, and age boundaries, these guides will enhance the lives of women in America as they empower them in their weekly devotions. The study guides can be used for both individual and group settings.

Women are asking good questions about their faith. With our study guides, we want to join them in their quest for knowledge and lead them in finding the answers they are seeking.